T0334073

Cambridge Elements ☰

Elements in the Problems of God
edited by
Michael L. Peterson
Asbury Theological Seminary

GOD AND THE PROBLEMS OF LOVE

Kelly James Clark
Ibn Haldun Universitesi – Philosophy

CAMBRIDGE
UNIVERSITY PRESS

CAMBRIDGE
UNIVERSITY PRESS

Shaftesbury Road, Cambridge CB2 8EA, United Kingdom

One Liberty Plaza, 20th Floor, New York, NY 10006, USA

477 Williamstown Road, Port Melbourne, VIC 3207, Australia

314–321, 3rd Floor, Plot 3, Splendor Forum, Jasola District Centre, New Delhi – 110025, India

103 Penang Road, #05–06/07, Visioncrest Commercial, Singapore 238467

Cambridge University Press is part of Cambridge University Press & Assessment, a department of the University of Cambridge.

We share the University's mission to contribute to society through the pursuit of education, learning and research at the highest international levels of excellence.

www.cambridge.org
Information on this title: www.cambridge.org/9781009462334

DOI: 10.1017/9781009269131

First published 2023

A catalogue record for this publication is available from the British Library

ISBN 978-1-009-46233-4 Hardback
ISBN 978-1-009-26915-5 Paperback
ISSN 2754-8724 (online)
ISSN 2754-8716 (print)

God and the Problems of Love

Elements in the Problems of God

DOI: 10.1017/9781009269131
First published online: November 2023

Kelly James Clark
Ibn Haldun Universitesi – Philosophy

Author for correspondence: Kelly James Clark, kclark84@yahoo.com

Abstract: Religious believers are often commanded to love like God. On classical accounts, God seems a poor model for human beings: an immutable and impassable being seems incapable of the kind of episodic emotion (sympathy, empathy) that seems required for the best sorts of human love. Models more conducive to human love, on the other hand, are often rejected because they seem to limit God's power and glory. This Element looks first at God and then divine love within the Abrahamic traditions—Islam, Christianity, and Judaism. It will then turn to love and the problem of hell, which is argued as primarily a problem for Christians. The author discusses the kind of love each tradition asks of humans and wonders, given recent work in the relevant cognitive and social sciences, if such love is even humanly possible. This title is also available as Open Access on Cambridge Core.

This Element also has a video abstract: www.Cambridge.org/Clark

Keywords: God, love, Islam, Christianity, Judaism

ISBNs: 9781009462334 (HB), 9781009269155 (PB), 9781009269131 (OC)
ISSNs: 2754-8724 (online), 2754-8716 (print)

Contents

1 *GOD* and Love

I don't remember what I did yesterday, but I recall like it was yesterday giving a class presentation on "God is love" in a secular philosophy class with a secular professor at a secular university in 1977. I was an undergraduate at Michigan State University, and I was in a philosophy class on logical positivism taught by H. G. Bohnert, one of the last living logical positivists.

Logical positivism, a most fashionable philosophy of the 1920s and 1930s, restricted factual knowledge to the sciences and just the sciences; they claimed that anything beyond sense experience is nonsense (roughly, whatever is "meta" (beyond) "physica" (physics) is nonsense). They "argued" that traditional metaphysics, the philosophical exploration of what is beyond sense experience, is meaningless. For example, while it's meaningful to say that the sun is at the center of our planetary system (heliocentrism) or that when closed containers are heated the pressure of the gas inside increases ($PV = nRT$), it's meaningless to say that the ideal of roundness or goodness exist in a perfect, nonphysical realm (Platonism). Moreover, since positivists believed that the reality beyond or behind our sense perceptions is unknowable, they likewise rejected such claims as "gas is composed of tiny particles scooting about rapidly" (aka atoms) as metaphysical nonsense. Now to the theological point: since God lies beyond the physical, all theological statements are nonsense. "God is love" is a prime example of metaphysical balderdash according to positivists.

As meaningless nonsense, God statements couldn't even rise to the level of true or false. Statements about God, according to the positivists, are as nonsensical as Lewis Carrol's intentional gibberish:

> Twas brillig, and the slithy toves
> Did gyre and gimble in the wabe

Saying "God is love," then, is like saying (literally), "The color purple ordered the roast beef with a side of mirth," or, again, "silence is golden but melancholy is greedy." Like Lewis Carrol's gibberish, such statements may provide amusement or provoke consternation, and they may make some sort of poetical or metaphorical sense (especially when cashed out into the language of science); however, as literal nonsense, they cannot be either true or false. Religious believers, on this view, are more silly than mistaken. As a Christian, I took offense.

I aimed my presentation mainly at unmasking the presumptions of logical positivism. Its cramped theory of meaning may have valorized the sciences, but it proclaimed as nonsense nearly everything else that humans believe, everything that makes life worth living. For example, if logical positivism were true, then the belief that *the killing of innocent children is wrong* and *Beethoven's music is beautiful* would be nonsense. And if positivism were true, central religious beliefs like "God is love" would be nonsense. Finally, I argued that the claim "only scientific statements are meaningful" is self-refuting because it, itself, is not a scientific statement.

At the conclusion of my presentation, Professor Bohnert, the last living logical positivist, clapped politely and then asked, "So what exactly do you mean when you say, 'God is love'?"

My twenty-year-old self, with passion exceeding understanding, stammered, "Ummm, ya know, I'm not sure *exactly* what I mean." Honestly, I wasn't even sure what I inexactly meant. I found myself saying, "Well, I think it means that God cares deeply for us but *not* in a way that means that God would or should prevent the holocaust or mosquitos or the drowning of an infant." I had just read John Updike's *Rabbit Run*, in which Rabbit, the main character, comes home to find that his drunken wife had accidently drowned their baby daughter in her bathwater. As he stares into the tub, still filled with the deadly water, Rabbit "thinks how easy it was, yet in all His strength God did nothing. Just that little rubber stopper to lift." Omnipotence evidently doesn't love in that lifting-rubber-stoppers-to-prevent-babies-from-drowning sort of way. At that time, I could only think of what I don't mean when I say, "God is love." So, I stammered some more, returned to my seat, and slumped down.

After working in the philosophy of religion for more than forty years, I'm still not exactly sure what I mean when I say, "God is love" (probably because I understand even less what I mean by "God" and "love"). Let me put it more precisely. I think I have some inkling of some of the various literal and more earthly meanings of human love – I've got some sense, when things go right, of what it means for a husband to love his wife, a parent her child, friends their friends, and a neighbor a stranger. I think that I've even had some first-hand experience of these various forms of human love. But I think I'm now even more perplexed about what it means to say that God is love – more perplexed about what I mean, what we mean, by "God" and "God is love." In this Element, I will discuss some of my perplexities.

Provisos. By selecting this text and that thinker and those issues and these responses (and not any number of other texts, thinkers, issues, idioms, and responses), I am constructing a narrative as much as relaying arguments. So I will inevitably tell *my* story of the problems of God and love; others, for sure, would have told a different story. Like the other Elements in this series, I will offer the basic essentials of the issues, the rudiments of the arguments, and a broad sense of the problems – as I see them; others, for sure, see them quite differently. Although there has been voluminous scholarly publication on many of the issue that I discuss, I will not footnote each jot and tittle; I don't want scholarly minutia to obscure the narrative. I will offer a representative text or set of texts that can serve for deeper and wider exploration. Moreover, every philosophical and theological assertion that I make represents the idea of some participant or set of participants in the relevant debates. And for each assertion, *p*, there is an equal and opposite asserter of *not-p* (and for good reason); again, I understand that not everyone involved in the discussion agrees with me (the reader should understand that eminently reasonable people disagree with me on nearly every point). When faced with such profound intellectual disagreement among sincere truth seekers, humility seems in order. To be clear, I do not mean to assert that those who disagree with me are per force irrational or crazy or immoral (though I think them mistaken). I say this forthrightly because in much discussion of religion and philosophy, disagreement is often allied with unwarranted derision and denigration.

While I will refer to classical thinkers such as Maimonides, Aquinas, and Averroes, I will be primarily referring to contemporary, analytic, philosophical thinkers and discussions.

Finally, I will try to write without assuming that every reader has a background in theology or philosophy (or the Abrahamic religions). As such, I will try to keep jargon to a minimum.

In a text on God and the problems of love, it behooves us to offer some definitions of "God" and "love." To prevent us from talking about, as Locke fetchingly describes matter, the "something we know not what," we need at least some preliminary understanding of our subjects. In this section, I'll discuss the nature of God. But before getting to definitions of God, let's take a brief excursus into just what definitions are and do.

Thinking and Speaking about Elephants

Sometimes we define something by offering a list of key properties of or ingredients for that thing. Sometimes we define by pointing. The first sort of *definition*, as philosophers typically understand these terms, is the *descriptive meaning*, the second sort of definition is the *referential meaning*.

For example, "elephant" might be defined as "the largest living land animal distinguished by a large trunk and two tusks." A complete descriptive definition of "elephant" would say much more, including average weight, evolutionary history, color, shape of skull, weight of brain, diet, and gestation period. But, for most practical purposes, the shorter and appropriately precise the better. What are the practical purposes of descriptive definitions? Descriptive definitions are used, by and large, in *thinking* and *communicating*.

Suppose you take your children to a zoo and they see an elephant for the first time. "What's that, Daddy," one asks. You tell her it's an elephant. "What's an elephant, Daddy?" You tell her that it's the largest living land animal distinguished by a large trunk and two tusks. Armed with her new understanding, she looks to her right and says, "Hey, there's another elephant!" Your daughter has gained a new concept – elephant – used it to cognize her perceptual experience and then to communicate with you. You beam proudly.

However, if your daughter is a thirty-two-year-old biologist, she may wish for more. When she's completed her studies, her definition of "elephant" may be something like "there are two species of the African elephant: *Loxodonta africana* and *L. cyclotis*, which evolved from the common ancestor, *Moeritheriums*; its prominent proboscis, used mainly to drink water, evolved in response to various selection pressures." And so on.

Such precise definitions, while unnecessary for 99.99999% of human contexts – unnecessary, that is, for elephant identification and human communication – are essential to the development of an intellectual discipline. When charged by an angry elephant in the bush, one needn't recall "there are two species of the African elephant: *Loxodonta africana* and *L. cyclotis*, which evolved from the common ancestor, *Moeritheriums*" before thinking and shouting, "Elephant. RUN!!!!" For most human contexts – identification and communication – a simple, ordinary descriptive definition is fine.

Given the varieties of human contexts and human uses of language, it follows that there's not just one, privileged, descriptive definition of "elephant." Moreover, most descriptive definitions are imprecise (but useful).

Suppose, as is not uncommon, that one's culture told "Just-So Stories" of the origin and nature of various animals. Consider Rudyard Kipling's, "The Elephant's Child," where one reads that elephants live nearabouts the banks of "the great grey-green, greasy Limpopo River" and were full of "satiable curiosity" and initially had no trunk (with a nose no longer than a boot). Elephants got their trunks, in the story, when the "satiably curious" Elephant's Child, against the advice of the other elephants, visited the Crocodile to ask him what he eats. "Come hither, Little One," said the Crocodile, "and I'll whisper." When he got close, the Crocodile grabbed him by the nose and tried to jerk him into the limpid stream and eat him. Although it "hurt him hijjus," the Elephant's Child pulled and pulled and pulled and his nose stretched and stretched and stretched until the Crocodile finally let go. And though he waited for it to shrink, the Elephant Child's nose grew no shorter. The story concludes: "For, O Best Beloved, you will see and understand that the Crocodile had pulled it out into a really truly trunk same as all Elephants have today."

I suspect that most humans for most of human history learned of the elephant and its distinctive size and trunk from similar Just-So Stories. And, though often wrong about locale, habitat, and trunk, such definitions served perfectly well for human identification and communication. The true etiology of elephants, much of which was deeply mistaken until the time of Darwin, would come hundreds of thousands of years later.

One might think then, and some philosophers do, that descriptive definitions are sometimes irrelevant. None of them – from the Elephant's Child's to scientific definitions – is especially useful in identifying or speaking about elephants. Humans for hundreds of thousands of years successfully referred to elephants without having heard Rudyard Kipling's story or having the slightest idea that elephants had genes at all, let alone that distinctive elephant genetic code. No particular description, not even a true description, is necessary to think and speak of elephants.

What, then, do definitions need to secure their meaning? Sometimes what's important for identifying and communicating is reference: a long time ago someone, somewhere saw an elephant and pointed to it, perhaps among a group of people, and said, "elephant" (or some early language equivalent). The original use(s) of the term, "elephant," involved no descriptions whatsoever. There was just a pointing and a naming (perhaps a grunting). And people got it. From then on, a community could communicate about elephants and everyone knew what everyone was talking about. What's important for meaning then? Reference.[1]

My professor asked, "What exactly do you mean when you say, 'God is love'?" More broadly, we might wonder, what *exactly* do we mean when we use *any* word? I doubt that we ever *exactly* mean anything. Yet, mostly through reference and sometimes through description, words serve their practical purposes of identifying and communicating.

Enough of elephants. What about God?

The Abrahamic God

Early human beings lived in a god(s)-haunted world. Just for starters, there were gods of rivers, gods of mountains, gods of weather, and gods of war. In the earliest Hebrew narratives alone (the Jewish *Tanakh*, which Christians call "the Old Testament"), we encounter, in addition to Jehova, Inanna, Anat, Nehushtan, Moloch, Baal, Baal Berith and Beelzebub, Chemosh, Jad, and Shapash (and many more). There were in the Hebrew narrative gods of cities and even gods of persons. Jehova, for example, was "the god of Abraham, Isaac, and Jacob" (likely to differentiate him from the gods of other people, tribes, and cities).

---

[1] I am following a line of thought developed by Saul Kripke (1980).

Only much later in the Hebrew narrative is it claimed that there is just one God and all of the others are mere wood and stone (idols). So the first problem when discussing *God* and the problems of love is which God (or, maybe, whose God)?

For purposes of this Element, I will be speaking of *the Abrahamic God*, perhaps more perspicuously *the God of Isaac, Jesus, and Ishmael* (considered the first progenitor of Muslims). I'm writing from the perspective of Western, Judeo-Christian-Islamic monotheism. I am speaking, by name, of Yahweh, G-d, Jehova, the Father, Allah, the Merciful and the All-Compassionate ("Allah" is the Arabic name for God, a name used by Muslims, Jews, and Christians alike in Arab-speaking communities). The Element may have been much different if I had decided to write about Hindu gods, or Buddhism or Sikhism or Taoism. But, given the paucity of my knowledge of, say, Hinduism and Sikhism, it would have been a decidedly weaker book. Best if I write about what I know.

Do Muslims, Jews, and Christians Believe in the Same God?

Second problem for *God* and love. Do Muslims, Jews, and Christians even believe in the same God? Given the rise of Christian nationalism, the reemergence of anti-Semitism, and the prevalence of Islamophobia, it's worth spending some time on this topic. Indeed, since we'll later discuss human love, it's worth noting that human failures to love are sometimes rooted in beliefs that other humans are impugning God's honor with their false beliefs about God and so, humans sometimes violently attack those with whom they disagree about God. See, for example, ancient Hebrew conquests of idolatrous nations, historic Christian anti-Semitism and recent Christian Islamophobia, and contemporary Islamic terrorism. Nonetheless, maybe, contra appearances, Muslims–Christians–Jews believe in the same God (if not in the exact same ways). Our discussion here will rely on insights gained concerning descriptive and referential meaning in the elephant section.

Suppose there is a God who a long, long time ago spoke to Abraham, promising to bless the world through his descendants. Suppose, beginning with Isaac and Ishmael, his descendants told their friends who told their friends, who told their friends about Abraham's encounter with God, with some of those friends later identifying as Jews, some as Christians, and some as Muslims. Their descriptions agree in many respects, even important ones – they all believe, for example, that God is one, merciful, just, and creator. Their descriptions of God also differ in some respects. Christians, for example, think that God was incarnate in Jesus, while Muslims and Jews reject the Trinity. And they, Muslims–Christians–Jews, sometimes call God different names – among them, Yahweh, the Father, and Allah.

Different names and different descriptions. No big surprise, really. Over the course of several millennia and with diverse linguistic groups, theological telephone is likely to produce a lot of variations among both descriptions and names.

But, I contend, if Muslims, Christians, and Jews believe in the God who spoke to Abraham, they believe in the same God. And, if Abraham was directly acquainted with God, they do. God's names and descriptions – same or different – are (mostly) irrelevant.

Many Christians, however, assume that belief in God crucially involves getting one's description of God exactly right.

Christians believe that God was incarnate in Jesus, the second person of the Trinity and that salvation is attainable only through Christ's atoning sacrifice on the cross. Muslims and Jews, on the other hand, believe that Jesus was a prophet (not God in the flesh) and that the doctrine of the Trinity violates Jewish and Islamic monotheism.

Different descriptions, different gods. Case closed.

Can two people believe in the same God only if they have identical or nearly identical descriptions of God? This assumption, which may seem obviously true, is flawed both philosophically and spiritually.

Two people can believe in the same God with incomplete, incompatible, and even false descriptions of God.

Let me offer a simple, non-God, example. Douglas Cone, of Tampa, Florida, was married to Jean Ann Cone and together they had three children: Julianne, Douglas, Jr., and Rammy. Douglas Carlson, of Tampa, Florida, was married to Hillary Carlson and together they had two children, Carolee and Fred. Both the Cone and the Carlson children attended the same school, Berkley Prep. Over lunch at Berkley Prep, friends Rammy Cone and Fred Carlson would sometimes speak fondly of their fathers.

In 2003, Tampa was shocked to learn that Douglas Cone and Douglas Carlson were one and the same person, with secret lives and wives. When Rammy and Fred were talking about their fathers in, say, 1999, they were, unbeknownst to themselves, talking about the same person. They both *knew* the same person but by different names and different descriptions. And both Rammy and Fred had *relationships* with the same person.

As long as both Rammy and Fred had both encountered the person variously called "Mr. Cone" and "Mr. Carlson," both were talking about and even relating to the same person. They related to the same person because both were directly acquainted with him, not because of or through their descriptions.

Their descriptions are not, of course, irrelevant. But the descriptions are irrelevant to the two of them relating to, talking about, and even knowing exactly the same person.

Relating to a person requires only that one be *acquainted* with that person, either directly or indirectly (through a chain of testimony that traces back to someone who was directly acquainted with that person). This is a good thing because most descriptions of most people are partial, mistaken, and even contradictory.

Back to God. Muslims–Christians–Jews believe in the same God if they are either *directly acquainted* with God (perhaps through religious experience) or part of a *chain of testimony* that traces back to someone who was directly acquainted with God (say, Abraham). Believing in the same God does not require any religious believers to get their description of God just right (or even right at all).

Here's another way of putting it. Acquaintance with Douglas (sometimes with the surname Cone, sometimes with the surname Carlson) is all that relating to and talking about Douglas requires. *Acquaintance with God* on the part of Muslims–Christians–Jews (either directly or indirectly, say through Abraham) is all that belief in the same God requires.

If Abraham was directly acquainted with God and told his children who told their children, who told their children, . . ., then Muslims, Christians, and Jews believe in the same God. Muslims, Christians, and Jews may worship in different ways, call God different names, and describe God differently (sometimes incompatibly), but they *believe in* the same God.

If I've made the case that when it comes to belief in God – that reference (acquaintance) is more important than description – then we can speak meaningfully of the Abrahamic God, the God of Isaac, Jesus, and Ishmael. I've offered a case, through referential definitions, that Muslims–Christians–Jews believe in the same God.[2]

Finally, and this is the spiritual issue, the religious believer should be grateful that one can believe in God without getting one's description of God just right. After all, given the plethora of beliefs about God, what are the chances that any of one of us has gotten God just right? We should hope for some generosity on God's part when it comes to getting our theology just right, and we should share God's generosity when we make judgments of other people's theology.

We've made a case that problem number 2 – that we can speak meaningfully of the Abrahamic God – has a solution. And now on to problem number 3 concerning *God* and the problems of love: we find within Judaism, Christianity, and Islam various and even competing views on *the nature of God* that have consequences for one's views of divine love. These problems arise within one's

---

[2] Many Christian theologians insist that believing in or referring correctly to God is not the real issue; the real issue is worshipping God, and worship is different among these traditions (according to many Christians, only Christians worship God in the right way). However, at this stage, I am only concerned with *belief in*, not worship of, God.

theology, one's *belief that* God is thus and so. Just as the biologist requires precise descriptive definitions, so, too, theological discussion requires precise descriptive definitions. *Belief in God* requires only knowledge by acquaintance, one's description of God can be flawed. But theological discussion involves claims that God, for example, does or does not have foreknowledge of the future or can/cannot change. Such claims involve descriptive definitions of God, definitions that have import for understandings of divine love.

Which God?

One year I undertook the project of reading the entire Bible from beginning to end and writing down exactly what it says about God. At the very beginning (in Genesis, "beginnings"), I jotted down that God doesn't know the future and doesn't even know everything about the present ("Where are you?", God asks of Adam in the Garden). Yahweh has regrets and upsetting emotions (Genesis 6:6). Yahweh changes, does not know the future, cannot do certain things, and is dependent on creatures (for emotional states and will). God suffers with us, for example, upon the occasion of the suffering of His children (upon hearing the cries of His people in bondage in Egypt). The future seems as open, unpredictable and even surprising to God as it is to human beings. As such, the theology associated with this description of God has been called *Open Theism*.[3] Finally, according to Open Theism, God responds to prayer, suffers in reaction to human hardships, and works in partnership with humans to carve out an unforeseen but hoped for future. The God of Open Theism walks with me and talks with me.

However, in my philosophy and theology studies, I encountered an entirely different God, captured in so-called *Perfect-Being Theology*.[4] According to Perfect-Being Theology, God has every good-making property and to the maximum. So God has the good-making property of knowing and to the max: God is omniscient (all-knowing); God has the good-making property of power and to the max: God is omnipotent (all-powerful); God has the good-making property of righteousness and to the max: God is perfectly good. And so on.

A maximally perfect being, I would also learn, is not only omnipotent, omniscient, and perfectly good; God is immutable and impassible.

God is *immutable*: God cannot change. Here's a simple argument for divine immutability. If God were to change for the better, then God would not be perfectly good, and if God were to change for the worse, then God would not be perfectly good; ergo, God cannot change.

---

[3] Defenses of Open Theism include Swinburne 1993, Pinnock 1994, Sanders 1998, Pinnock 2001, and Hasker 2004.

[4] Defenses of Perfect-Being Theology (classical theism) include Helm 1994, Flint 1998, Craig 2000, Rogers 2000, Frame 2001, Geisler and House 2001, Ware 2001.

God is *impassible* means that God cannot suffer upsetting emotions (*pathos*); God, on this view, is in a state of perpetual bliss (*apathos:* lacking pathos or upsetting emotions).[5]

Perfect-Being Theology is also often associated with strong forms of *divine sovereignty* whereby God has complete control over all events in the world; this typically entails a correspondingly less robust form of human freedom. The God of Perfect-Being Theology is high and lifted up.

So does God walk with me and talk with me (and work with me to create a better future) or is God high and lifted up (watching in bliss as His perfect plan for the world unfolds)? Open Theism or Perfect-Being Theology?

Blaise Pascal distinguished between *the God of Abraham, Isaac, and Jacob*, on the one hand, and *the God of the Philosophers*, on the other. Let us take these to track Open Theism and Perfect-Being Theology.

As I'm taking it, the God of Abraham, Isaac, and Jacob is God, more or less, literally revealed in the Bible – the God who does not have complete knowledge of the future, the God who is disturbed by human suffering and even suffers with us, and the God who is empathetically moved to act compassionately in response to unforeseen but desperate situations. The God of Abraham, Isaac, and Jacob is the God of Open Theism. Open Theism carries with it its own problems and prospects. Open Theists, for example, claim the following benefits:

- Robust views of human freedom.
- Significant role of human beings working with God to accomplish God's purposes.
- Fit with piety; we need a God who suffers with us and who hears our prayers.
- A natural reading of the Bible (let God tell us who God is).
- Moral evil is wholly attributable to created, free persons.

Its critics allege the following problems for Open Theism:

- God takes risks (re: human salvation, the outcome could be low).
- We want a God not so overcome by emotion that God cannot act in our best interest.
- We don't want a God who accedes to finite, self-interested human prayers.
- Anthropomorphism threatens to create God in our own image.
- Diminishes God's sovereignty and even God.

The God of the Philosophers, on the other hand, abides in a state of eternal bliss, unperturbed by the suffering of His creatures, acting on our behalf through the inevitable unfolding of His divine plan, unsurprised and unmoved by human

---

[5] For a book-length discussion of impassibility, see Creel 1985.

suffering (Wolterstorff 1988). The God of the Philosophers is the God of Perfect-Being Theology.

Perfect-Being Theology, one might think, takes the Bible as a sort of Just-So Story about God – a tale offered to primitive peoples that no longer should be taken literally in its details. As *revelation progresses*, again one might think, God is increasingly revealed as high and lifted up, outside of time, and in complete control of His creation – a maximally perfect being, one might think. God didn't actually suffer with His people just as the croc didn't actually pull the elephant's nose. But as elephants have elongated trunks, God cares for His creation. Such stories serve for practical purposes. But for the sober, metaphysical truth about God, one must reject the Bible's Just-So Stories and rely on the construction of Perfect-Being Theology. Defenders of Perfect-Being Theology take the biblical language of divine change, pathos, and partial knowledge to be *anthropomorphism* – wrongly describing the nonhuman in human terms. According to this view, God imparts information about His nature by *accommodating* Himself to the cognitive limitations of His finite and contingent creatures.

As with Open Theism, Perfect-Being Theology has its prospects and problems. The benefits of Perfect-Being Theology include:

- Divine providence is meticulous: God's purposes will be exactly fulfilled in every detail.
- God's love, goodness, and faithfulness cannot be lost or changed.
- God accords with our best philosophical ideas of perfection.
- God has a reason for every evil.

But these alleged benefits are bought with a price; critics claim that according to Perfect-Being Theology:

- Meticulous providence diminishes human freedom.
- An impassive and immutable being is distant, unmoved by human suffering, hypercontrolling, and unresponsive to prayer.
- Philosophical views on perfection impose a theology contrary to God as revealed in Scripture.
- God, as the ultimate source of all things, is implicated in evil.

Which, then, is more true? The God of Abraham, Isaac, and Jacob or the God of the Philosophers? Open Theism or Perfect-Being Theology?[6] To be perfectly honest, I have no idea (and I have no idea how either the Open Theist or the

---

[6] Given the purview of this Element, I have been more focused on raising problems than offering solutions to the problems. I have raised each problem for Open Theism and Perfect-Being Theology as an allegation; as such, I am not asserting that I think each problem is equally

Perfect-Being Theologian can be certain of their views; settling one's views of God is a massive hermeneutical, theological, and philosophical problem). Nonetheless, and this is important: although they offer radically different, even contradictory descriptive definitions of God, both Open Theism and Perfect-Being Theology refer to and – like Muslims–Christians–Jews – believe in the same God. Moreover, Open Theism and Perfect-Being Theology share many beliefs about God – that God is a good, for example, creator and providential. Of course, at least one of them is wrong about some of God's properties. In one sense, so be it. You don't need a correct description of God to successfully refer to and believe in God.[7]

God and Love

In this discussion of *God* and love, focusing as I am on God, I restricted myself to the Abrahamic traditions. I argued that Muslims–Christians–Jews *believe in* the same God – the God of Isaac, Jesus, and Ishmael. For *belief in God*, I argued that reference by acquaintance is sufficient (assuming that God revealed Himself to Abraham, who told his children [Isaac and Ishmael], who told their children, who told their children, etc.). Then I moved on to claims about the nature of God, *belief that God* is Open or Perfect. Such descriptions of God, also known as "theology," are more precise manners of speaking. Just as scientific inquiry requires increasingly detailed and precise descriptions (of, say, elephants), so, too, theological inquiry requires increasingly detailed and precise descriptions of God.

But precise definitions, theologies, of God raise substantial problems. For example, some claim that the God of the Philosophers (Perfect-Being Theology) is rooted in biblically foreign, a priori philosophical and theological reflection. The God of Abraham, Isaac, and Jacob, on the other hand, is rooted primarily in more literal interpretations of Holy Writ. Is God maximally perfect (omniscient, omnipotent, outside of time, impassible, in complete control, etc.)? Or is God inside of time, limited in knowledge and power, in indirect and incomplete control, and so on? Each of these definitions of God has its own intrinsic problems and, I will argue in the next section, raises problems for understandings of divine love.

---

challenging (or without reply). Each of the claims of benefit and cost have been addressed by the various defenders of the various positions. I invite the interested reader to follow out the debates in the primary texts.

[7] Contemporary discussion of Open Theism and Perfect-Being Theology has been mostly restricted to the Christian academic community. I would be remiss, however, if I didn't note Abraham Joshua Heschel's biblical defense of the divine pathos in the Jewish tradition (Heschel 1962).

I won't settle the issue of which God–Open Theism or Perfect Being Theology–in this Element (or anywhere else). I won't settle because I don't know. And I doubt anyone else really knows. However, different conceptions of God create different problems for love, human and divine. So I'll explore various conceptions of God and the problems of love, rather than settling on any one particular theology.

2 God and *LOVE*

In the previous section, I focused on understandings of God's nature. In this section, I will focus on understandings of God's love. One might think that there are no problems understanding God's love. After all, according to Perfect-Being Theology, God has every perfection to the max; love is a perfection; therefore, God has love to the max. No problem. But problems arise in one's understandings of God's love based on one's concept of God. For example, some Perfect-Being theologians hold that God has no feelings; if love is a feeling, then God cannot love (or must love in some other, very different way).

On the other hand, Scriptural references concerning divine love portray God as loving us like a father loves his children or a lover his beloved. So one might think that God loves us like a Father or Lover (only, unlike earthly fathers and lovers, perfectly). Again, problem solved. Such inferences are widely rejected by the most famous thinkers within each of the three Abrahamic traditions as *anthropomorphism* (as misattributing human properties to a nonhuman thing or object).

I will raise two of the most serious problems concerning divine love – the Immutability–Impassibility Problem and the Negative Theology Problem – for Perfect-Being Theology and show how just one view of divine love – benevolence – comports well with the nature of God as prescribed by Perfect-Being Theology. I will then discuss the problem of transcendence for any view of divine love. I will then raise the Anthropomorphism Problem for Open Theology. But let me first speak of love.

Love in the Abrahamic Traditions

"Love" in the Hebrew Bible is the English translation of a wide variety of Hebrew terms, including *aheb*, *hasad*, *raham*, *yada*, *dawad*, *yad*, and *yada*. In the New Testament, written in Greek (though Jesus spoke Aramaic), we find *agape*, *phileo*, and *storge*. And in the Quran, Islam's holy book, *hubb* and *ishq* are the terms mostly widely translated "love." In context, these terms refer to a wide variety of phenomena, including romantic attraction, desire, lovingkindness, devotion, sex, sexual desire, the beloved, cuddling, compassion, empathy, and acts of mercy. If we omit the passages in which "love" refers to sexual desire, cuddling, and desire more generally (like "I love chocolate"), love in each of the three traditions seems to mean one of two things. I'll call them, for sake of simplicity and comprehension, *benevolence* and *compassion*.

Love as *benevolence* is willing and acting for the good of others. Benevolence, note, refers only to *willing* and *acting*; it says nothing about feelings. While we, in the West, associate love (especially romantic love) with a feeling or feelings, benevolence focuses simply on intention and action. Out of love, one intends to act for the good of others and then acts for the good of others. You might look at it this way – even if you despise the stinky beggar, love requires you to intend and to act for the beggar's good. How you *feel* about the beggar is irrelevant.

Love as *compassion* includes willing and acting for the good of others (benevolence) but adds something like *empathy* into the mix. Empathy involves feeling with and for another person because of his or her suffering; empathy may even include participating in the suffering of another. The apostle Paul, for example, exhorts us to "rejoice with those who rejoice; mourn with those who mourn" (Romans 12.15). Empathy involves a deeply felt concern for the good of others. Peter, for example, counseled Christians to have "compassion for one another; love as brothers, be tenderhearted . . . " (I Peter 3:8). In the Quran, we read of the Prophet's empathy: "Grievous to him is what you suffer; [he is] concerned over you and to the believers is kind and merciful" (Quran 9.128).

The Abrahamic traditions also hold that a deeply felt concern for others is rooted in respect for others. So the Abrahamic traditions hold that our highest acts of love are empathetic and respectful responses to the needs and suffering of others. I use "compassion" as the best term to unite both empathy and respect with right action. The highest form of Abrahamic love, compassion, is when we see or sense another's needs and our hearts move us to act to satisfy those needs.

What we mean by "others" is a matter of discussion. While the father's love for his child and romantic love are often models or metaphors for love, love in the Abrahamic traditions is aimed at more than spouse and kin. I will develop this point further in Section 4. In the meantime, I will simply note that each of the three Abrahamic traditions insists on *love of everyone* – from one's child spouse and neighbor, on the one hand, to the stranger and even enemy on the other. No one, each tradition teaches, is or should be immune from the respect and empathy that move us to act for the other's good.

God Is Love

The Scriptures of the Abrahamic traditions trade on human and earthly models and metaphors to describe God's love and loving nature. God is the Potter and we are the clay, the work of His hand (Isaiah 64:8). God loves and cares for His children like a father (and, sometimes, a mother). We are the sheep and God is our Shepherd (John 10:1–18); as Shepherd, God cares for us, provides for us, and protects us. We are, the Gospel of John teaches, God's friends (John 15:15). And we are the bride and God is the Bridegroom (John 3:29); as Bridegroom, God pursues and woos the bride in hope that we choose Him.

Jewish and Christian founding texts share a common metaphor of divine love – God as Father (Jeremiah 31:9; Isaiah 64:8; Proverbs 3:12; Matthew 6:9; Romans 8; Luke 11:12). The father–child metaphor of divine love, again a dominant theme in the Hebrew Bible, includes empathy: "As a father has compassion on his children, so the Lord has compassion on those who fear him" (Psalm 103.13). Fathers, when things go right, use caring discipline and nurturing love to raise up their children to flourishing adults. These texts likewise offer female images of divine love (Isaiah 66:13, 49:15; Matthew 23:37). Female images of the human–divine relationship explicitly affirm a profoundly and deeply intimate love relationship, different from the stereotypical father–child relationship, of God for His children.

The Quran is full of human-like images of the divine. For example, God has eyes, ears, hands, and face; God sits on His throne; God talks and listens. And although the ninety-nine names of God don't mention "Father," they include names that are reminiscent of ideal father-like and mother-like care and concern. God is, to mention just a few of His ninety-nine names in the Quran, the Most Merciful, the King, the Giver of Peace, the Guardian, the Restorer, the Originator, the Fashioner, the All-Forgiving, the Giver of Gifts, the Most Appreciative, the Most Generous, the Protector, and the Giver of Life.

Finally, the holy texts of the Abrahamic traditions portray divine love both in the mode of benevolence and in the mode of compassion. It is not difficult, in any of the founding texts, to find representations of God willing and acting for the good of others. Indeed, God's very way of being, as described in these texts, is willing and acting for the good of others. We also find God moved to act by affective, empathetic attitudes toward His creatures – that is, we find God the Compassionate.

Perhaps the most famous of God's empathy-motivated actions is found in the opening chapters of Exodus in which God frees His people from their bondage in Egypt. In the New International Version, we hear the LORD speaking to Moses: "I have indeed seen the misery of my people in Egypt. I have heard them crying out because of their slave drivers, and I am concerned about their suffering" (Exodus 3:7). God, moved by their suffering, determines to "come down to rescue them from the hand of the Egyptians and to bring them up out of that land to a good and spacious land, a land flowing with milk and honey."

In the New Testament, we read of the empathy of Jesus, "the visible image of the invisible God." In the Book of Hebrews, we read of the ascended Jesus, our great high priest, "For we do not have a high priest who is unable to empathize with our weaknesses, but we have one who has been tempted in every way, just as we are – yet he did not sin" (Hebrews 4.15). The empathy of the second person of the Trinity grounds divine mercy and grace "in our times of need."

Nearly every chapter in the Quran begins with just two of God's ninety-nine names: "In the Name of Allah, Most Merciful, Most Compassionate." "Mercy" and "compassion" are English translations of variations on the Arabic *rahmah*, which shares the same root (*rahim*) with "womb." As such, *rahmah* and its variations connote a mother's selfless care, affection, and compassion for her children. In a famous Hadith, it is reported the Prophet was aware of a woman who selflessly nursed the babies of prisoners of war. The prophet's comment: "Allah is more merciful to His servants than this mother is to her child." Allah's empathetic care extends, according to the Quran, to all of creation: "My *rahmah* has encompassed everything" (Quran 7:157).

Divine love, as represented in the Abrahamic texts, is most essentially compassion (as I've defined it). Compassion, by definition, includes benevolence – intending and acting for the good of others. Divine love at its finest also includes empathy – feeling with and for another person because of his or her suffering, and then acting to relieve that suffering.

Divine compassion, again as represented in the Abrahamic texts, occurs in response to the suffering and needs of God's creatures. As such, compassion is episodic – it depends on temporally specific episodes of suffering and need such as the suffering of the Hebrews in Egypt or the starving of motherless babies. Compassion, then, is the disposition to sense and share another's suffering or feel another's needs which moves one to act to fulfill those needs. One may have the virtue of compassion, but if one is never aware of suffering or need, one could never become emphatic (just as one might be courageous but never face any danger). The virtue of compassion, like the virtue of courage, is engaged by temporally specific and appropriate events in the world.

Yet, as I will show in the next two sections, the greatest thinkers in each of the Abrahamic traditions would deny that divine love is compassion, with some rejecting the notion that God has any feelings or emotions whatsoever. God, according to these great thinkers, loves only in the mode of benevolence.

Love and Immutability–Impassibility

Although the Scriptural texts of the three Abrahamic traditions affirm compassion – empathy moved into action – as the highest form of love, both human and divine, their greatest thinkers affirm views of God which would make divine compassion impossible (Oord 2022). Maimonides and Gersonides, Augustine and Aquinas, and al-Ghazali and Avicenna concur: God as immutable and impassible cannot change and cannot have any episodic or upsetting emotions. As noted in the previous section, empathy is both episodic and upsetting. Empathy is engaged in response to events in the world, and empathy's shared feelings of suffering are likewise upsetting. But impassibility precludes the possibility of episodic and upsetting emotions.[8]

According to the doctrine of immutability, God does not and, indeed, cannot change. The argument for divine immutability is as follows:

1. God is perfect and perfectly good.
2. Any change would be for the better or the worse.
3. God can't change for the better (b/c God is perfect).
4. God can't change for the worse (b/c God is perfect).
5. Therefore, it is impossible for God to change.

I leave this argument without comment and will just discuss its consequences for divine love.

If God cannot change in any way, then God cannot change with respect to the episodic knowledge and feeling states that engage empathy. Empathy is typically taken to have two aspects – cognitive and emotional. *Cognitive empathy* involves taking another's perspective by imagining what it might be like to be in their situation; one might, intellectually, understand what someone else is feeling. *Emotional empathy* involves sharing in another's emotional experience, usually feeling distress when you see that person in pain. A compassionate person will allow that shared feeling to move them to action to relieve the other's suffering or pain. Compassion, then, requires two changes in a person, a change in one's cognitive and in one's emotional states. If one's actions were to relieve the suffering, this would occasion another cognitive change in the empathetic person – knowledge of suffering relieved and sharing in the delight or joy of the previously suffering person. Again impossible, on the face of it, for a being that cannot change in any way.

If God is immutable, so it seems, God cannot love in the mode of compassion.

However, an immutable God *might* feel another's episodic pain. How so? An immutable (and foreknowing) God might know of such pain and even feel such pain but not episodically or mutably. For example, although my grief over the suffering and death of my mother waxed and waned over a period of time in the early 2000s, God may have eternally and timelessly suffered with me. An immutable God can

---

[8] For defense of both sides of the impassibility issue see Creel 1985, Helm 1990, Weinandy 2000, Gavrilyuk 2004, and Matts 2019.

grieve; if so, unlike any human creature, God grieves eternally and immutably. And if an immutable God can timelessly and eternally feel our pain, then an immutable God can timelessly and eternally love in the mode of empathy.

Although an immutable being may (immutably and eternally) suffer or grieve in response to happenings in the world, an impassible being cannot.

Divine impassibility is variously defined as the doctrine that (a) God is not affected by happenings in the world, (b) God cannot suffer any upsetting emotions, and (c) God cannot suffer (Creel 1985). Although everything in the world is dependent upon God, God is not dependent upon or affected by anything. The Council of Chalcedon in 451 AD declared *Patripassionism*, the claim that God the Father suffers, a heresy when it proclaimed that the synod "repels from the sacred assembly those who dare to say that the Godhead of the only-begotten is capable of suffering."

God might be impassible in any number of ways – in nature, will, action, knowledge, and feeling or in any combination thereof. Nearly every Abrahamic theist – Open Theist and Perfect Being Theologian alike – believes that *God's nature* is immutable; they hold that God is, for example, omnipotent, omniscient, and perfectly good and cannot not be omnipotent, omniscient, and perfectly good. God's nature cannot be changed or affected or diminished or augmented in anyway whatsoever.

But is *God's will* impassible? Can God's will be influenced by forces outside Himself, say by our suffering? Open Theists contend that if God responds to changing circumstances that are temporally located (suffering in Egypt, say, or starving babies), then God must continually adapt His will to these changing circumstances. So the impassibilist holds that suffering does not change God because God is necessarily and timelessly adapted to the future. Perhaps God is like an omniscient chess master whose knowledge of chess is so vast that he never improvises or deliberates. God the Chess Master has planned for every eventuality – whatever happens, God has already timelessly willed His action. God, on this account, need never decide His response to our actions after we have performed them (Flint 1998).

Critics of divine impassibility (Mullins 2020), however, argue that even if God's decisions were eternally determined, he would need to implement those decisions at the right times and in the right places; hence, *God's actions* must be passible. However, it may be possible for Omnipotence and Omniscience to decide and even act eternally. God's actions may be like a giant computer program with all of God's responses "built in" from eternity: if so and so occurs, then God, timelessly and eternally, responds thusly. God can be impassible, so it seems, with respect to both willing and acting (Stump and Kretzman 1981).

The tug toward *possibility*, the belief that God is responsive to the suffering and needs of God's creatures (and is thus dependent in some ways on creatures) is nowhere stronger than with respect to *God's feelings*: divine love and suffering. Does love require emotional passibility? Is it necessary that a loving being rejoice with those who rejoice and mourn with those who mourn? Does love entail joy in the joy of another and sorrow in the sorrow of another? Must God be angry at times of injustice and sin and pleased during times of obedience? Is the highest love a suffering love, so a lack of suffering love would imply a lack in divinity?

Impassibilists reject any logical connection between love, loss, and suffering. God's response to our suffering is tempered by both God's knowledge of the world redeemed and God's power and determination to redeem. While I might suffer as my uncle suffers in the final stages of terminal cancer, God sees my uncle's suffering redeemed; God sees my uncle through his new life in paradise (with his character perfected through that suffering).

Again, I might suffer if my child gets hit by a car and breaks all of her bones, but I am impotent and cannot fix my daughter. God, on the other hand, has the power to fix what I cannot – God can, for example, fix my daughter so that she dances gloriously in paradise. God, so it seems, should suffer with us only if He knows that we have suffered an unfixable evil or have lost an irreplaceable good. But for the Abrahamic theist, all evil is fixable; therefore, there is no reason for God to become vexed over our temporary setbacks. God views our sufferings *sub specie aeternitatis* (from the aspect of eternity). On the other hand, we suffer sometimes because our perspectives are temporal and finite (we'd suffer less if we were more aware and convinced of God's astonishing power to fix).

I will not settle here whether or not the impassibilist or the passibilist has the better view. I will only note: if God is impassible, then God (a) is not affected by happenings in the world, (b) cannot suffer any upsetting emotions, and (c) cannot suffer. And if (a), (b), and (c), then God cannot love in the mode of compassion. Compassion requires empathy, and empathy requires being affected by happenings in the world (suffering in Egypt, say, or starving babies), suffering upsetting emotions (pity, say, or sorrow), and suffering (with).

If God is impassible, then God cannot love in the mode of empathy.

If God cannot love in a way that requires empathy, then, God loves in the mode of benevolence. God wills and does good things for us, perhaps all that is necessary for our salvation, but God does not suffer with us.

What kind of emotional life does God have then?

God is happy, on the impassibilist view, in part because divine grief is impossible. Moreover, if God is complete unto Himself, then God's nature includes everything God requires for happiness; after all, God didn't need to create the world. It's not as though God got lonely and decided His life would be better if He created people to alleviate His loneliness. Since God lacks nothing, God desires nothing; as such, God can neither lack nor be disappointed; God's life is a life of uninterrupted bliss (Wolterstorff 1988). Although human beings are enjoined to suffer sympathetically with other human beings, God's life is *uninterrupted suffering-free bliss*. Hence, God's love manifests not in compassion but in benevolence.

Here's a way to unsympathetically understand divine benevolence. God has a steady disposition toward our good, so God has willed everything necessary for our good. God is undisturbed by events in the world and incapable of suffering with those who are suffering. As His people suffer as slaves in Egypt, for example, God is in a state of undisturbed and undisturbable bliss. God's bliss is unsullied even when observing Hitler and the Holocaust. Slavery, holocausts, even the destruction of the planet cannot disturb God's bliss. If every single human were to suffer eternal torment in hell, God's eternal bliss would be unaffected; God's happiness may even be augmented by the fact that God loves His creatures (willed everything necessary for their salvation), even if not a single creature were to avail him- or herself of God's good-doing.

What I've just presented as a problem, others would claim as a virtue of divine impassibility. After all, no one wants a weepy, wimpy God who is hostage to the ravages of our world. Just as we want a doctor who is wise and capable and not blinded by emotion, even moreso do we want Ultimate Reality to be omniscient, omnipotent, immutable, and impassible – God's job, after all, is to heal the world, not to weep at its shortcomings. Our God is a conquering God.

I leave this debate, these caricatures, at this point. I have shown enough, I think, to demonstrate the impassibility–immutability problem for one's view of God's love.

The *Via Negativa*

Abrahamic thinkers affirm the oneness of God. In so doing, they affirm that (a) there is just one God (all other "gods" are unreal idols) and (b) God is a metaphysical unity (sometimes called "the doctrine of divine simplicity"). We will look at the consequences of (b) for one's understanding of divine love. If God is a metaphysical unity, then any ascription of attributes that imply that God is a plurality is deeply mistaken (Dolezal 2011). God is not a substance with the attributes of omnipotence, omniscience, and goodness tacked on. God is one. There is no distinction in the One between subject and predicate. So our common understanding of God as plural – as a subject with tacked-on properties – is wrong and even misleading. As such, God is unlike anything else in creation because everything not God is a plurality of substance and properties. God is not like anything in creation.

Here's another way of putting it – any attempt to say *what God is* is nonsense. Every saying of *what God is* treats the One as a plurality. Although we cannot say what God is, we can say *what God is not* (not like anything under the sun). Thinking we can speak only of what God is not has many names: negative theology, the *via negativa,* apophatic theology.

One might also think that *God is transcendent*: God is so far above humans and the creation, so utterly different, so Wholly Other, so Holy (separate from) that God is unknowable (because no human or creational or finite attributes could possibly apply to God).

Finally, *the problem of anthropomorphism* rears its ugly human head for Open Theism. Open Theists take very literally (some of) the human and earthly attributions of God. For example, God is, we read, a rock, a fortress, a deliverer, a refuge, a shield, a horn, and a stronghold. But no one believes that God *is* a rock, a fortress, a deliverer, a refuge, a shield, a horn, or a stronghold; God is, under any interpretation and by any interpreter, *like* a rock, a fortress, a deliverer, a refuge, a shield, a horn, or a stronghold. Rock, fortress, deliverer, refuge, shield, horn, or stronghold are metaphors for God, used to communicate that God is steadfast, a source of comfort, and a sounder of warning.

What about the more human metaphors? Open Theists beware: God is not a big human being; though the Scriptural texts proclaim, God does not literally have eyes or ears. God knows everything but without eyes or ears. And while God is all-merciful, God is only *like* a father and a mother. Unlike our fathers, God did not have sex with our mothers (as our biological fathers did) or rock us to sleep at night or shake us awake in the morning (as my father did). God does not literally breastfeed us. God is not father or mother.

What, then, *is* God shorn of human-like metaphors and images?

Suspicion is aroused: perhaps we cannot know what God *is* at all. If we cannot know what God is, the best we can say, is what God is not. According to the *via negativa,* then, theology proper is the study of *what God is not* (Williams 2021).

Scriptural support for the *via negativa* can be found in each of the three traditions. For example, in the Hebrew Bible, God's ineffable name (essence), the unspeakable, "I am who I am," is revealed to Moses. Moreover, God's ways are unsearchable and unfathomable (Job 11:7-8). Jewish thinker Maimonides thought that finite, human language is so inadequate to describe God's infinite nature, one could aspire only to respectful silence. According to St. Paul, God, whose essence is beyond our cognitive grasp, "lives in unapproachable light, whom no one has seen or can see" (I Timothy 6:16). Finally, the Quran (in 42:11 and other texts) asserts that there is nothing in creation or creatures that is like God. There is, Islamic tradition would come to hold, no similarity whatsoever between the creator and His creation in essence, attributes, or actions. God, in Islam, is beyond all human concepts of Him.

According to the *via negativa,* we cannot say that God is good, we can only say that God is not or cannot commit evil (or, in God there is no evil). We can say that God is unlimited (not limited), infinite (not finite), indivisible (not divisible), invisible (not visible), and ineffable (not describable in words). Omnipotence is the claim that God is not impotent (not limited in power), omniscience is the claim that God is not limited in knowledge.

According to the *via negativa,* we cannot literally say that God is omnipotent, omniscient, and perfectly good. What about the Abrahamic affirmation that God is love? If God's essence is ineffable and unknowable, what can be meaningfully asserted of divine love? Surely the Abrahamic traditions mean more, much more even, than "God is not hate."

I will simply conclude this section noting this – if God is unknowable and ineffable, then we have no understanding whatsoever of "God is love." I take that to be a problem for Abrahamic theology.

Transcendence and Love

God transcends the limits of human language, true enough. Yet this statement can taken a radical turn that implies that it is impossible to speak meaningfully about God at all. This turn was inspired by the philosopher Immanuel Kant, who drew a sharp distinction between reality as we humans experience it (shaped by our human conceptual framework) and reality as it is in itself. John Hick, for example, draws a sharp, Kantian distinction between the Real as it is in itself and the Real as humanly experienced; we have cognitive access, according to Hick, only to the Real as humanly experienced; the Real as it is in itself is mystery (Hick 1985).

The boundaries of meaningful human discourse, according to the Kantian theologian, are determined by empirically available concepts – those that categorize what we can see, hear, touch, taste, or smell (concepts like "is blue," "tastes sweet," and "feels hot"). Since God cannot be captured by empirically available concepts, all talk about God trivializes and tempts one to blasphemy. God/God's essence lies completely beyond all human attempts to grasp it. Radical transcendence, if true, is an avenue to the claim that God is ineffable and unknowable.

The theological consequences of this Kantian view are extraordinary. We cannot know if God is loving or hateful, righteous or wicked, concerned or unconcerned about human welfare, or even person or thing. Behind the veil of human language is, again to use John Locke's fetching phrase, something we know not what. Some theologians have gone so far as to claim that it is inappropriate even to think of God as existing, as that would locate Him as just another being among all other beings (of course, one wonders if they mean to ascribe to God the opposite of existence, which ascription, so it seems to me, would have severe consequences for theology!).

Is God so Wholly Other that we are invariably reduced to uttering and thinking nonsense concerning God's nature? Is God so Wholly Other that humanly available concepts of love simply don't apply?

Let us distinguish two senses of "transcendent." A being is *radically transcendent* if that being is not humanly graspable because humanly available predicates do not apply to that being. If God is radically transcendent, then it is impossible to conceive of God at all.

But another definition of "transcendent" is possible: a being is *modestly transcendent* if that being is partially but not fully graspable by human concepts. A being is modestly transcendent if we cannot *fully* understand that being. One's understanding of a modestly transcendent being will prove, to various degrees, inadequate. Such a being transcends in the sense of going beyond whatever descriptive terms are predicated of it.

Rocks and persons are modestly transcendent (no finite human understanding of a rock or a person can fully grasp a rock or a person) but nonetheless partially comprehensible. Thus, a being may modestly transcend experience but nonetheless be (at least partially) comprehensible. Our experienced slice of reality is slim, but slimness of grasp does not entail skepticism about reality, possibly even divine reality.

A central theological problem for divine love is whether or not God is radically or modestly transcendent.

If God's transcendence implies that God is totally hidden and unknowable, as in radical transcendence, then we can know nothing of God's love.

If God is modestly transcendent, it might be possible to know something (but surely not everything or even close to everything) about God's love.

Consider a rock. The rock modestly transcends any mental conception that we have of it. Were we to devote our lives to the study of that one rock we would only grasp a minute bit of it. Were we to stare at it for days, each moment our perspective would be limited to one of the countless moments and perspectives from which to view the rock; and we lack access to all prior and future presentations of the rock. Its essence, its inner construction, its history, and its future are all absent from our finite experience of the rock. The rock modestly transcends our experiences of it. So our idea of the rock, an enduring substance of countless unexperienceable permutations, is a partly mental construct. We start with our finite, transient experiences and add to them existence outside of our minds, location in space and time (if Kant is right), persistence in the absence of our perceptions, and so on. The rock cannot be identified with any of our experiences of it or even our complex idea of it. All of this is unquestionably true. Our minds are actively involved in the cognizing of the rock as it categorizes in ways that vastly exceed our pale and frail immediate experiences.

How about a person, say Ray? Ray, like the rock, modestly transcends any of my ideas of Ray. Ray, of course, is more complicated than a rock and his complications increase the pressure of transcendence; in addition to having outer, physical properties, which are not completely accessible to any finite knower, Ray is a person and has a characteristic inner life of thoughts, desires, and emotions. But I can't see Ray's thoughts, feel his emotions, or sense his desires. The problem of other minds looms large – other minds are in principle beyond what humans can experience. Nonetheless, Ray is a person, who persists through time, and who has experiences and an inner life beyond that which any person (including Ray) could fully grasp. But it doesn't follow that my idea of Ray captures nothing of the real Ray; my limited perspective does allow some limited, modest access to truths about Ray.

And, finally, what of God? Suppose there is a God. Is it possible for human beings to grasp truths about God or does divine transcendence make that impossible? If Kantian theologians are right, no one could know anything about God's nature, about the Real in itself. Are they right?

I don't know of any nonquestion begging manner of settling this matter. Let me suggest, however, a possible way of proceeding. If we have been created in God's image, then we share some divine properties. It has been suggested that we are icons of God in that we are free, rational, moral, creative, social, and knowers; if so, then God has similar properties. Yet, very likely, God infinitely transcends any human grasp of them.

Consider God's causal powers: His causal powers vastly exceed those of mere humans; God is able to directly bring about vastly more states of affairs than human beings. Yet God is creator in the sense that God intends for something to be that isn't and then brings it about that it is. And so do humans. God, however, creates without using any preexisting stuff. Humans create pottery and paintings out of clay and oil and paper. God, on the other hand, creates universes out of nothing. Humans and God are both creators, but are almost infinitely different in intention and ability.

So, too, God is a knower; God has beliefs. Unlike humans, all of God's beliefs are true, and the domain of divine beliefs is unrestricted and infinite; God knows everything about everything. We, of course, know a little about a few things. Perhaps God knows everything directly whereby we acquire many beliefs by inference or testimony or reasoning. Humans and God are both knowers, but are almost infinitely different in domains and extent and modes of acquisition.

And God is good, although His superiorities of knowledge and power render the actions expressive of divine goodness vastly different from those required of humans.

I don't intend to defend a particular view of God-talk. I only mean to suggest that if one reasonably believes that we are icons of God, then one may reasonably believe that God has some properties which are somewhat like but vastly exceed those possessed by humans: God is modestly transcendent. If we are created in the divine image, then we share some properties with God; as such, we might share, finitely and modestly, some divine properties.

To be sure, the plurality of incompatible properties ascribed to God (by apparently sincere truth seekers) and our awareness of the self's desire to believe what is to one's and one's tribe's advantage suggest the likelihood of humans to err in their understandings of God and so cautions us not to indulge in triumphalism, dogmatism, or overconfidence. Modest transcendence warns us not to turn our feeble beliefs about God into an idol or to use God as a weapon.

Nonetheless, God may be like both rocks and persons in this one respect: rocks and persons exceed my cognitive grasp, and God exceeds my cognitive grasp. But we can know something of rocks, persons, and gods. So rocks, persons, and gods are modestly transcendent. But modest transcendence does not entail that we cannot know anything at all about rocks, persons, and gods.

I don't mean to suggest that there are no unique difficulties involved with talk about God. God is not just like a rock or a person; God vastly exceeds both. But if God is modestly transcendent, then although we can know little about God, we can also know a little about God. That shouldn't come as a surprise: we also know little about rocks and persons, yet we can know a little about rocks and persons. Of course, we almost certainly can know vastly more about rocks and persons than God.

Rather than entailing skepticism about God, though, one may affirm both knowledge of God and of human cognitive limitations; after all, although rocks and persons transcend our piddly conceptions of them, we can still know and relate to rocks and persons.

Affirming modest transcendence places us securely in the tradition of some of the greatest Abrahamic thinkers. Augustine, for example, held that God is like a vast ocean: the unlearned can paddle about in the shallows and the trained theologian can swim out a bit further, but both are of such limited ability that they would be swallowed up in the depths. Aquinas contended that because of the disproportion of our finite intellect and God's infinitude, our knowledge of God is "dark and mirrored and from afar." Soren Kierkegaard maintained that there is an "infinite qualitative difference" between humans and God and that humans, due to their sinful nature, are tempted to domesticate God to make Him serve them. Each of these thinkers affirmed divine transcendence yet also held that we can know enough about God to relate to Him properly.

God is *modestly* transcendent – we can gain sufficient information to relate to God; but God is *transcendent* – we must beware of the human temptation to turn God into a glorified human being or an omnipresent buddy. Modest transcendence is a threat both to the theological liberal who wallows in utter ignorance of the divine and to the theological conservative who arrogantly asserts and perhaps wields such knowledge to divide and conquer. The Abrahamic theist holds that we can embrace or be embraced by God but only as chastened by intellectual humility.

I have belabored this discussion of transcendence to these ends: (1) If God is radically transcendent, then we cannot ascribe the property of love to God. (2) If God is modestly transcendent, then it *might* be possible to ascribe the property of love to God. (3) If we are created in God's image, then we may ascribe something *like* some human concepts of love to God. All big ifs, but ifs enthusiastically affirmed in the Abrahamic traditions. Finally, (4) modest transcendence, while possibly providing sufficient knowledge to relate to God and to each other, would preclude arrogance and idolatry; as such, God should not be domesticated or nationalized to serve one's own or one's tribe's selfish ends. Indeed, one might think modest transcendence could help ground both a theological understanding of love and the humility necessary for spreading human love beyond self and tribe.

Suffering Love

Given the Abrahamic endorsement of compassion as the highest form of love, is it sufficient for God to have merely a steady disposition to do good for His creatures? Is God's love, to put the matter another way, equivalent (limited?) to benevolence? If so, then, contra the plain reading of their Scriptures, God delights only in His own well-doing, not in the welfare of His creatures. Indeed, God takes delight only in His disposition to do good, regardless of the condition of His creatures or of their responses to His love. Since His desires are not directed toward His creatures but are focused only upon Himself, God's happiness is not affected by their sin and suffering. Is benevolence an adequate conception of divine love?

One might think, to return to caricatures discussed previously, that the ideal doctor would, on the one hand, be extremely competent and, on the other hand, care. And one might hope that the doctor is motivated, at least in part, by her care and concern. Finally, one might hope that the doctor would rejoice in her patient's healing and mourn their sickness and death. Of course, one does not want the doctor's feelings to overwhelm the doctor's professional competence. One might want the doctor to grieve inside, not through teary eye that blurs her healing vision; the ideal doctor controls her grief. And if a doctor, tired and overwhelmed, can't rustle up any care and concern, then that doctor should love in the mode of benevolence; but that seems to reduce the doctor's "care" more to duty than to love. That's fine, of course, in terms of outcomes – the health of the patient. But it's not a model of love at its highest. The ideal doctor loves in the mode of compassion, not crippling concern but proper act-motivating, patient-respecting feeling.

The highest form of love is compassion.

If God's love for His creatures is compassion, then God has desires for His creatures *and* their well-being. If God's desires are unsatisfied when human beings sin or suffer, then God's compassion is suffering and suffering-with love (Fretheim 1984; Wolterstorff 1988).

The impassibilist might respond that God, being omnipotent, need not live in fear that God will not attain His ends regarding human beings. God, after all, has determined to attain His ends and will do so because omnipotent. Since all human sufferings may be fixable and since God views all things *sub specie aeternitatis*, God can remain in a state of perpetual bliss. From God's eternal and timeless perspective present, suffering may be transformed because of the good now present to God. God may not view suffering as we do – we may suffer if a loved one suffers because the good that such suffering engenders is not now present to us.

For example, when a woman gives birth to a child, she suffers terribly, but in retrospect the suffering is forgotten and seems worthwhile. Yet, while she is suffering, the good is not yet fully present to her. Perhaps God's perspective on suffering is like a woman's later perspective on childbirth where the good now present transforms her attitudes toward her suffering. If God sees the end from the beginning, viewing all things in the eternal now, His redemptive viewpoint may see all present suffering through its attendant good. In this manner, God's viewpoint may enable Him to view human suffering without suffering Himself.

Such a Stoic picture of a desire-free God in a state of perpetual, uninterrupted suffering-free bliss seems incompatible with the biblical portrait of God; the biblical writers portray God as rejoicing and suffering over the state of creation and God's creatures. Moreover, as noted, God is sometimes portrayed as lacking foreknowledge of future human events. And the fate of both humanity and the world seems to hang in the balance, even to God. Finally, God seems to exist in time. Every good defense of Open Theism walks one through these relevant biblical texts.

Let's proceed backward this time. If God's love is compassionate, suffering-with love, what other attributes would God have?

First and foremost, if God suffers with us on the occasion of our own sufferings, then God's emotional and cognitive life change in response to human events. Hence, God cannot be immutable.

If God's emotional life is upset or disturbed by events in the world, then God cannot be impassible; God does not live in a state of eternal, suffering-free bliss.

If God does not know our human futures, and so doesn't know if His good-doing will produce its desired end, then God lacks exhaustive foreknowledge of the future. If humans have significant free will, a will that cannot be caused or coerced without violation even by omnipotence, then God might not know our human futures.

Some Abrahamic thinkers, on the other hand, hold that not only is God omnipotent (all-powerful), God is the only power (*monergism*); there are no independent sources of causal power in the world. On this view, even so-called free human choices are ultimately powered, caused, by God. But if humans have significant free will, then there are causal power sources independent of God (monergism is false).

Moreover, God may, like us, need to wait and see how human beings freely respond to God's good-doing. If God can or must wait to see human responses, then God does not exist outside of time (God is not eternal); God, if all of this is right, is inside of time.

You get the picture. If God's love is compassion, God, it seems, must be a passible, mutable, and temporal power-sharer. And God's inner life includes suffering and suffering-with.

Have we settled the issue in favor of Open Theism?

This discussion sets up the greatest criticism of Open Theism from the Perfect-Being Theologian: we've just made God in our own image (Geisler 1997). According to some Perfect-Being theologians, the Open God is ignorant, irrational, wishy-washy, wimpy, and even immoral. Open Theism, so such critics argue, is excessively anthropomorphic – applying human terms and concepts where they don't apply. After all, God clearly does not have literal ears or a mouth or a butt (for sitting on a literal throne). So why think God has literal emotions or is literally ignorant of the future? Such anthropomorphic texts can all be explained (away) in favor of Perfect-Being Theology. Finally, God is not like us or anything in creation. According to the Quran, there is nothing in creation like God; God vastly exceeds our human and creational constructs. According to Islam and Christianity, God is Holy, set apart from creation, completely unique, and distinct. God is not, as Open Theism would have it, a big human being.

I won't settle any of these debates – debates involving Scriptural hermeneutics, the regulative role of traditions over theology, the influence of philosophy on theology, the importance of free will, issues of transcendence, the limits of human language, and so on. These debates are flavored differently in each of the Abrahamic traditions (and even within each tradition). But I think I have shown enough to show some of the problems involved in conceiving of God's love. If Perfect-Being Theology is true, God loves in the mode of benevolence (but not compassion). If Open Theism is true, God loves in the mode of compassion (as well as benevolence). If nothing can be affirmed of the divine nature or if we can only speak of what God is not, then we have no understanding of divine love at all. And if God is radically transcendent, humanly available concepts of love cannot apply to God.

Affirming that God is love on any understanding of God and love, then, involves affirming a whole lotta ifs.

3 Love and Hell

Hell

David Hume, in his *Dialogues Concerning Natural Religion*, raises the classical problem of evil from Epicurus: "Epicurus's old questions are yet unanswered. Is he willing to prevent evil, but not able? then he is impotent. Is he able, but not willing? then he is malevolent. Is he both able and willing? whence then is evil?" Hume then goes on to outline typical examples of human misery and pain in the world including, among many others, "a hospital full of diseases, a prison crowded with malefactors and debtors, a field of battle strewed with carcasses, a fleet foundering in the ocean, a nation languishing under tyranny, famine, or pestilence." Evils such as these, Hume contends, are evidence against divine benevolence.

Yet examples of human misery and pain in this life pale in comparison with the Christian depiction of divine punishment in the next life, that is, in hell. According to the Christian Scriptures, hell is eternal conscious torment that vastly exceeds anything humans could possibly experience in this life. Hell is a "furnace of fire" (Matthew 13:50), "where their worm does not die, and the fire is not quenched" (Mark 9:48). If disease and famine and pestilence give reason to doubt divine love, eternal conscious torment in a furnace of fire without reprieve gives vastly more reason to doubt divine love. The problem of human suffering – the apparent conflict between human suffering and divine love – is dramatically amplified by the Christian doctrine of hell. How could it possibly be true that God loves His creatures and that God permits or even causes the eternal torment of the damned?

Conflicts between God's love and the doctrine of hell arise only on certain versions of the doctrine of hell. Jewish and Islamic views of hell seem relatively unproblematic given their views of divine justice and mercy. Christians, on the other hand, have a massive problem reconciling their views on hell with divine love.

Contemporary Jews, I've come to learn, think very little of the doctrine of hell, both in terms of time spent thinking and in terms of negative evaluations of eternal damnation. Jews are considerably more concerned with how God wants us to live in this life – a life of justice and flourishing and obedience – than preparing for and worrying about the world to come. Jews who do believe in hell typically hold that either humans live on in some shadowy netherworld (between this life and heaven), or that one passes through Sheol as purgative preparation for heaven.

Muslims, on the other hand, are deeply concerned with the afterlife, and their commitment to divine justice is reflected in their views of the afterlife. After death, God will justly judge each individual according to his or her deeds, with the righteous faithful moving on to reward in paradise and wicked infidels moving on to just punishment in hell. In Islamic thought, while the suffering in hell is physical, psychological, and spiritual, it varies according to the sins of the condemned person. Since human sins are finite, many Muslims believe that confinement in hell is temporary. And, since God is merciful, many believe that God will eventually eliminate hell. Finally, some Muslims think that after their period of just punishment, the all-Merciful will restore all humans to paradise. In short, the belief that God is just and all-merciful, temper Muslim understandings of hell. Indeed, Islam may offer the most perfect fit between Islamic understandings of the divine nature and the afterlife.

Christian views on hell, however, are difficult to reconcile with any reasonable understanding of divine love.[9]

Christian doctrines of hell, of the eternal and unrelenting torment of the damned, are based on seemingly plain Scriptures, especially the teachings of Jesus in the gospels. According to the Bible, punishment in hell is physical, spiritual, and everlasting. Hell is like a burning fire, the damned are separated from God and other humans (from all sources of light and life) forever. For example, the rich man in Hades, tormented by unquenchable fire, implores Father Abraham to mercifully send beggar Lazarus to dip his finger in cool water for relief; Father Abraham, in this story told by Jesus, rejects such a minor mercy, claiming that hell is a great chasm which no one can cross (Luke 16: 19-31). In the Revelation of John, we

---

[9] See Crockett 1997 for four views on hell. Defenders of hell include Swinburne 1983, Walls 1992, and Kvanvig 1993; I am not aware of any contemporary philosophical defenders of the traditional eternal, torture chamber view of hell. Critics of hell include Adams 1993 and Talbot 1999.

repeatedly hear "for ever and ever" concerning the punishment of the damned. Finally, the Christian Scriptures assert that considerably more people will end up in hell than in heaven: the gate that leads to destruction is wide and broad, the gate the lead to life is narrow and difficult and few find it (Matthew 7:13-14). Moreover, while some passages suggest that Satan and his minions will inflict the suffering (thus removing God one distance from hell), in other passages, God Himself seems to be the one inflicting the punishment. Hell, according to traditional Christianity, is a place where the wrath of God is poured out on sinners for an eternity; it is a place of torment, condemnation, judgment, and weeping and gnashing of teeth.

Medieval thinkers embraced the biblical metaphors of hell. Augustine contends that the tortures of the damned are both physical and spiritual and that the damned, who should be consumed by physical fire, are kept in existence by God Himself. Aquinas rejects the notion that the damned are tormented solely by fire, arguing that a variety of tortures will be employed. The term "fire" is prevalent in Scripture to describe the intensity of the pain, not the specificity of the torture. Eternal suffering, likened to the horror of being burned, is inflicted by torment "in many ways and from many sources" and without respite.[3] Indeed, hell will be so arranged "as to be adapted to the utmost unhappiness of the damned," and there will be, Aquinas argues, just enough light to perceive "those things which are capable of tormenting the soul" (*Summa Theologica* Suppl. Q. 97, Art. 5). One will, for example, see the corporeal fires and smell their stench as they burn one's corporeal body. This never-ending fire, Aquinas believes, is sustained not by fuel but by the breath of God.

We have heard enough, I think, to understand that the traditional Christian doctrine of hell – of God, in His wrath, punishing humans in the worst possible ways and forever – creates a problem for Christian understandings of divine love.

Love

Let us interpret God's love in a manner analogous to human love – as analogous to the ideal parent-child relationship; God is love, according to this analogy, as a father or mother loves his or her children. I don't pick this understanding of divine love out of a hat. As noted in the previous section, caring for one's child is a paradigm Abrahamic metaphor of God's care for His creatures: within Abrahamic holy writ, God is called and even named "Father," and examples abound of God's paternal care for creation and human creatures.

This view of divine love creates a special, perhaps unovercomeable problem of hell. I am assuming, for the sake of argument, the traditional, Christian eternal torture chamber view of hell, perhaps with God Himself as the torturer. Assuming that God loves us like a father his children, and the Christian eternal torture chamber view of hell, the problem of hell is that

1. God is love.
2. There is a hell.

are logically incompatible. In the next few sections, I will present some medieval(ish) ways of reconciling (1) and (2). I will argue than none is successful. Since many contemporary Christians maintain the traditional view of hell, this is a contemporary as well as a medieval problem.

Medieval Theories of Divine Goodness

Medieval attempts to reconcile God and hell typically assume an understanding of existence – *existence is good* – to justify God's keeping the damned in existence forever even given their horrific suffering. In short, the good of their existence outweighs the suffering of the damned (or the good of their (suffering) existence outweighs the bad of their nonexistence). God loves the damned, then, by maintaining their existence. And, properly informed, the damned would agree. I shall paint the medieval Christian tradition with broad strokes. It is not my intention to offer careful historical exegesis. Rather, I am interested in gleaning a rough consensus from medieval thinkers about the goodness of existence, one that aims at reconciling the suffering of people for eternity with divine love. I will focus primarily on the works of Augustine and Aquinas.

Aquinas contends that "being" and "goodness" are interchangeable. Being and goodness, according to Aquinas, are transcendentals; they transcend the categories; they don't serve as properties which categorize anything since they apply to everything. Everything has being and is good. To exist is good; so, everything that exists is good.

How does Aquinas establish the connection between being and goodness? How does he argue that "Goodness and being are really the same"? Very roughly and briefly, his argument may be put as follows:

1. To say that something is good is just to say that it is desirable.
2. Something is desirable to the extent that it is perfected.
3. Something is perfected to the extent that it is in being.[5]
4. Hence, something is good to the extent that is in being.
5. Hence, goodness and being are the same (*Summa Theologica* Ia.5.1).

I shall leave this argument without comment, simply noting that it is representative of the views of divine goodness of many medieval thinkers (and many contemporary Thomists).

Every being *qua* being is good. Lesser existents share in the divine goodness by participating in the highest good: "God is good through His essence, whereas all other things are good by participation. . . . Nothing, then, will be called good except in so far as it has a certain likeness of divine goodness. Hence, God is the good of every good" (*Summa Contra Gentiles*, Bk. 1, ch. 40). Everything that exists participates in the divine goodness. By participation, everything gets its being from God; goodness and being are convertible. Hence, everything that exists participates in goodness. "Everything is called good," Aquinas writes, "by reason of the similitude of the divine goodness belonging to it . . . " (*Summa Theologica* Ia.6.4). That everything is good led Augustine to develop and Aquinas to affirm the doctrine of evil as the privation of the good – evil is a mere shadow of existence and does not really exist.

God loves, then, by allowing things to participate in God's existence (i.e., goodness). Aquinas defends the view that God loves by virtue of imparting existence, ergo goodness, to a multitude of things:

> . . . the communication of being and goodness arises from goodness . . . Now each thing acts in so far as it is in act, and in acting it diffuses being and goodness to other things. Hence, it is a sign of a being's perfection that it can "produce its like" . . . That is why it is said that the good is diffusive of itself and of being. But this diffusion befits God because . . . being through Himself the necessary being, God is the cause of being for other things. God is, therefore, truly good. (*Summa Contra Gentiles* Bk. 1, ch. 40, art. 3)

God loves God's creatures by bringing them into and maintaining their existence; by virtue of sharing God's existence (goodness), God grants humans the honor of existing.

God's Goodness to the Saints

It is not difficult to reconcile divine love with God's treatment of the saints. According to Aquinas, the suffering of the saints is turned into a good that benefits the sufferer. God works everything for the good of those who love Him. According to Aquinas this means:

> Whatever happens on earth, even if it is evil, turns out for the good of the whole world. Because as Augustine says in the *Enchiridion*, God is so good that he would never permit any evil if he were not also so powerful that from any evil he could draw out a good. But the evil does not always turn out for the good of the thing in connection with which the evil occurs, because although the corruption of one animal turns out for the good of the whole world– insofar as one animal is generated from the corruption of another–nonetheless it doesn't turn out for the good of the animal which is corrupted. The reason for this is that the good of the whole world is willed by God for its own sake, and all the parts of the world are ordered to this [end]. The same reasoning appears to apply with regard to the order of the noblest parts [of the world] with respect to the other parts, because the evil of the other parts is ordered to

the good of the noblest parts. But whatever happens with regard to the noblest parts is ordered only to the good of those parts themselves, because care is taken of them for their own sake, and for their sake care is taken of other things . . .. But among the best of all the parts of the world are God's saints . . .. He takes care of them in such a way that he doesn't allow any evil for them which he doesn't turn into their good.[10]

God does not use the saints as instruments to the good of either Himself or other people or things. Rather the suffering of the saints is a means to the good of the one suffering.[9]

Augustine holds similar although less explicit views on human suffering. According to Augustine, "All other punishments, whether temporal or eternal, inflicted as they are on every one by divine providence, are sent either on account of past sins, or of sins presently allowed in the life, or to exercise and reveal a man's graces" (*City of God* XXI.13). Even the suffering of the apparently innocent is a means to a good end – suffering can detach us from undue reliance on the things of fortune and attach us to God, our ultimate satisfaction in the world to come: "Is innocence a sufficient protection against the various assaults of demons? That no man might think so, even baptized infants, who are certainly unsurpassed in innocence, are sometimes tormented that God, who permits it, teaches us hereby to bewail the calamities of this life, and to desire the felicity of the life to come" (*City of God* XXII.22).

According to both Augustine and Aquinas, the suffering of the saints redounds to their own benefit. Presumably *these* benefits could not have obtained without precisely *that* suffering. What are the benefits? Evils, both natural and moral, could free us from devotion to the self and thus enable us to develop humility, pry our fingers from clinging to the transient goods of this earth and orient our character toward eternity, make us aware of the limitations of self-sufficiency, and urge us to seek divine assistance. All suffering, at least for the saints, is pedagogical.

Finally, God loves the saints by sustaining them in eternal, blissful existence (after a life of suffering). God loves the saints like children – God permits only such harms as God can turn into their good, for fulfillment of their nature: growth in virtue and eternal participation in their highest good, God Himself.

God's Love for the Damned

But what about unbelievers? How does God love them? All things work together for the good of those that love God, but what about them that don't? Do all things work together for their harm? One might think so, given medieval

---

[10] From Aquinas's commentary on Job. As quoted in Stump (1993).

views of the nature of the eternal destiny of the damned. God, it appears, does not love the damned. But such an inference is resisted.

How can God love the damned? If goodness is identical with being, then God can love the damned simply by allowing them to exist. God loves them, recall, by virtue of creating them. As Aquinas writes:

> . . . God loves all existing things. For all existing things, in so far as they exist, are good, since the being of a thing is itself a good . . .. Now it has been shown . . . above that God's will is the cause of all things. It must needs be, therefore, that a thing has some being, or any kind of good, only inasmuch as it is willed by God. To every existing thing, then, God wills some good (*Summa Theologica* I, 20.2)

God loves the damned by maintaining their existence (because existence is good . . .).

Augustine argues that existence is sufficiently good that it outweighs the suffering of the damned: "And truly the very fact of existing is by some natural spell so pleasant, that even the wretched are, for no other reason, unwilling to perish; and, when they feel that they are wretched, wish not that they themselves be annihilated, but that their misery be so." (*City of God* XI, 27). Here the argument assumes that the natural impulse to exist, which often prevents people even in the most wretched circumstances from committing suicide, persists in those who suffer in hell. Indeed, it persists in such a fashion that it outweighs their desire not to exist given their sufferings.

But Augustine seems mistaken. Suppose we grant that people would prefer to exist rather than not and that, hence, what people in hell desire is not annihilation of their existence but annihilation of their suffering. It seems clear, however, that no reasonable person would desire the continuation of eternal torment, what Augustine refers to as "the dreadful pains of eternal fire," to nonexistence. If one were appraised of one's situation – that unspeakable torment vastly beyond any *ante mortem* suffering will continue without ceasing – one, if one's personality has not already totally disintegrated, would reasonably prefer nonexistence to existence. Even if one were not fully aware of the duration of the sentence, surely no reasonable person would rationally choose to continue such suffering. The negative induction – "I have suffered thusly for a hundred or a thousand or a million years, maybe I will continue to suffer thusly for another hundred or a thousand or a million years" – is sufficient to rationally overwhelm one's desire for continued existence. People do, after all, choose suicide to eliminate their suffering of this life. It seems that reasonable people would choose annihilation over the infinite perpetuation of the "dreadful pains of eternal fire."

Existence alone does not seem sufficient for God to love the damned if they are suffering according to the medieval understanding of hell. Surely such persons could say, with warrant, "it would have been better for me if I had never been born." Existence is not so great a good that it could reasonably overwhelm any desire for nonexistence under any conditions, including those the medievals attribute to the damned in hell. I shall return to this shortly.

Retribution?

I will very quickly address the claim that divine love and eternal torment can be reconciled by appeal to retributive punishment. How, one might wonder, can God be loving and permit or inflict intense pain and suffering for eternity? The immensity and duration of the pain and suffering are often justified by appeal to retributive justice: the damned merit this sort of punishment because of their sins. Of course, their sins seem prima facie deserving of less than eternal torment. Some lying here, a little adultery there, a spell of petty theft here, a bit of coveting there. Surely, the punishments merited by these finite offenses add up to a sum considerably less than eternity. Even the worst of sinners, Hitler say, might deserve 100 years per person killed; supposing he killed 20 million people, Hitler would retributively merit 2 billion years of punishment – a long, long time but still considerably less than eternity. *What earthly sins could merit eternal torture?* And this addresses just the duration of the punishment, not the intensity of the pain and suffering.

The medieval justification of eternal torture casts human sins in a different light than suggested in the previous paragraph. The sin, according to this view, is ultimately not against mere mortals but against God Himself. Since God is infinite, retribution is infinite. The punishment (eternal torture) fits the crime (sin against Infinity).

God's parental love, it should be noted, would not preclude retributive punishment simpliciter; a good parent could punish retributively (simply because the child deserved it). However, a good parent's first inclination toward a disobedient child is punishment as pedagogy. A good parent would, to the best of their ability, arrange a punishment that would assist the child in properly orienting their will and subsequently their actions toward their flourishing. In some cases, however, the child might merit more punishment than would be strictly required for rehabilitation. In other cases, the child might be intransigent and remain obstinately opposed to rehabilitation. In both cases, the good parent might justifiably punish their child simply because she deserved it (retribution). It should be noted, however, that punishment as rehabilitation is the preferred option for parents; retributive punishment is the fallback option. Any good parent would prefer to mete out punishment that redounded to the benefit of their child rather than simply repaying their child for the harm done.

A loving God, then, would punish His children for rehabilitation first and retribution second. Retribution would be justified only if punishment were merited beyond what is necessary for rehabilitation or if God's children were intransigent. Moreover, since God is essentially loving, God's love would continue *post mortem*, with the desire to rehabilitate *post mortem* God's children and return them to Himself. There's little reason to think that Omnipotence would or could be frustrated by the relative obstinacy of unbelievers at death. Only if human character were to become decidedly fixed in vice would a loving God give up and exact retributive punishment.

Although retributive punishment is not incompatible with divine love, eternal torture as retributive punishment is. In retributive punishment, the wicked person is repaid harm for harm and no further. In Scripture, retributive justice was limited by "An eye for an eye, a tooth for a tooth," which would prevent exacting retributive punishment beyond the harm inflicted. The guilty merit exactly the harm they inflicted. To justify infinite torment, there must be infinite harm inflicted. But how could a finite human being over a finite period of time inflict infinite harm on finite humans?

Medieval theologians believe that the harm the guilty inflict is infinite because their sin is essentially against the Infinite God. Suppose it's true that when I stole that candy bar from the store so many years ago, I was sinning against God and not just the store owners (to the latter, I owed a dime or so). In sinning against God, even the Infinite God, has God been harmed?

It seems clear that God simply cannot be harmed in that way. Human beings can inflict a great deal of harm on other human beings, nonhuman animals, the environment and even themselves – partly because these are the sorts of things that can be harmed. But God, by God's nature, cannot be harmed. When we lack faith, defy God, or commit blasphemy, it is only, a *façon de parler* to say that God is offended. God is not harmed by our unbelief or blasphemy, *we* are. Unbelief and disobedience are bad for humans not for God.

That God cannot be harmed is implied by Perfect-Being Theology. If God is impassible, immutable, etc., then God is ontologically independent of human beings; God remains in a state of unperturbed and unperturbable bliss regardless of our sins. Because of God's nature, God cannot be harmed. And if God cannot be harmed, then we cannot offend God. And if we cannot offend God, then we cannot be guilty of an infinite offense against the Infinite God. Thus, we cannot merit an infinite punishment for that so-called infinite offense. Retributive justice is an untenable justification of the eternal torment of the damned.

Hell, on the traditional Christian view, is not for rehabilitation. There is no benefit to the sufferer other than the good of existing; and existence, I have argued, is not sufficient to outweigh the harm of the suffering. Loving parents may sometimes allow harm to their children, but only to the extent that they have the power to benefit the child. A loving God's increased ability to harm His children is tempered by His increased ability to rectify the situation in a manner that benefits the sufferer. If there is no outweighing good that benefits the sufferer, then the loving parent cannot allow the suffering. Others might benefit from the suffering of those in hell: those in heaven might see their narrowly missed fate and be even more grateful to God for their rescue. Indeed, Aquinas thinks that the flourishing of the saints in heaven is due, in part, to their enjoyment of the suffering of the damned: "That the saints may enjoy their beatitude and the grace of God more abundantly they are permitted to see the punishment of the damned in hell." But no earthly parent could be loving and allow harm to come to one of their children simply for the good of another of their children. Children cannot be used merely as a means to the (good) ends of other children. If God were to allow some to suffer in hell for the benefit of those in heaven, He would not be loving in any sense related to earthly parents. Our sense of divine love would bear no resemblance to our human sense of love (the only sense of love that we have).

Eleonore Stump's Theodicy of Hell

I've argued that if God loves us like a parent loves her child, divine love is incompatible with Christianity's traditional doctrine of hell. Contemporary philosopher Eleonore Stump, who (rightly) rejects the traditional torture chamber view of hell, offers a new and more plausible defense of God's love and the doctrine of hell (Stump 1986). Drawing on insights from Aquinas, she defends the view that God is loving to those who suffer in hell. Although a vast moral and theological improvement, I will argue that Stump's view is still problematic.

Stump, following Aquinas, contends that "love for human persons consists essentially in treating them according to their nature; . . . God's love for a person involves helping to maximize that person's capacity for reason" (Stump 1986: 192). Stump defends Aquinas's conception of love and shows how it entails what we might call "tough-love" – Tough-God is not a pleasure-maximizer with respect to His children; God, while respecting their nature as autonomous and rational creatures, "promotes in them moral actions, emotions not contrary to reason, and in general virtuous states of character" (Stump 1986: 193).

Stump's theodicy involves a revision of the traditional doctrine of hell. What I call "revision," Stump calls a "closer look." I suggest that my term is more appropriate as she defends on an ameliorated view of hell inspired by Dante, not Augustine's and Aquinas's divine torture chamber view. Even so, I shall argue that it would not be loving of God to permit people to suffer in hell for all eternity even if hell were as Dante conceived.

One can imagine why Stump prefers Dante's view to Augustine's or Aquinas's. To maintain that the eternal existence of the damned is consistent with divine goodness, one must hold that persons in hell would reasonably choose eternal existence (over nonexistence) under those conditions. This would require, as I've argued, a substantial alteration in the medieval torture chamber view of hell. It is difficult to imagine anyone reasonably preferring eternal existence in such an unrelievedly, maximally painful state. If one were deprived of God, given any Abrahamic understanding of God and persons, it is difficult to imagine that one would or could bear to go on living in hell.

Stump, on Dante's view of hell, imagines that people may reasonably prefer eternal existence apart from divine grace because God has permitted the eternal willing of their preferred finite good – say lust, greed, or the desire for power – in place of the infinite good for which we are created (God Himself). Since people in hell "have become habituated to irrational acts" (Stump 1986: 195), God gives the damned what they want. While conceding that the vices of the damned are destructive of their nature, Stump contends that God wills to treat them according to their self-imposed "*second* natures" – now as lustful, say, greedy, or power-seeking beings.

Stump, following Aquinas on being and goodness, rejects the notion that God would or could be good by annihilating such beings:

> ... to eradicate being on Aquinas's theory is a prima facie evil, which an essentially good God could not do unless there were an overriding good which justified it. Given Aquinas's identification of being and goodness, such an overriding good would have to promote being in some way, but it is hard to see how the wholesale annihilation of persons could produce or promote being. In the absence of such an overriding good, however, the annihilation of the damned is not morally justified and thus is not an option for a good God. (Stump 1986: 196)

God is faced with a dilemma: He can't annihilate the damned and He can't work to fulfill their proper natures. Stump's solution: God treats the damned according to their second natures. He prevents them from harming the innocent, so keeping them from further evil, and he prevents any further degeneration of their character which would entail a loss of being. God can, within these limits, "maximize their being by keeping them from additional decay" (Stump 1986: 197). She concludes: "[God] treats the damned according to their nature and promotes their good; and because he is goodness itself, by maximizing the good of the damned, he comes as close as he can to uniting them with himself – that is to say, he loves them" (Stump 1986: 197).

I have, of course, omitted much of value in Stump's important contribution to a theodicy of hell. Nonetheless, I believe that I have faithfully presented the heart of her argument. Does Stump's theodicy preserve God's love in the face of the eternal suffering of the damned? Does Stump's theodicy offer an adequate account of hell and divine love? I think not. Let me offer two reasons to reject Stump's view.

First, the annihilation of the damned, even on Stump's Dantean view of hell, is rationally preferable to their continued existence. Aquinas himself concedes that there are some goods that result in a reduction in being. Indeed, these goods are just those involved in the relief of the suffering of the damned. He writes:

> *Not to be* may be considered in two ways. First, in itself, and thus it can nowise be desirable, since it has no aspect of good, but is pure privation of good. Secondly, it may be considered as a relief from a painful life or from some unhappiness: and thus *not to be* takes on the aspect of good, since *to lack an evil is a kind of good* as the Philosopher says (*Ethic.* v. 1). In this way it is better for the damned not to be than to be unhappy. . . . In this sense the damned can prefer *not to be* according to their deliberate reason. (*Summa Theologica* Suppl. Q. 98. Art. 3)

Aquinas contends that because it is a reduction in being (hence, goodness), *not to be* is (*prima facie*) evil; but *not to be* is also a good when it reduces unhappiness. Hence, *not to be* may be rationally preferable given one's circumstances. If *not to be* may be rationally preferable in certain circumstances, then surely those who are suffering in hell are in such circumstances. Hence, their continued existence alone, unless outweighed by a greater good, is not sufficient for God to be good to them. Arguably the good that Stump endorses, the good of fulfilling one's second nature, is not such a greater good.

Second, even supposing that it is logically possible for people to fulfill their "second nature" in a level of hell that contains only like-minded people, it is unlikely that this could become actual. Most vices require successful completion for their fulfillment. It is not enough to lust; one's desires must eventuate in actions for their fulfillment. If the happiness of the damned were, to turn Aristotle upside-down, (successful) activity in accordance with vice, then the modicum of flourishing permitted the damned would require the successful activity of one's vicious desires. If one were restricted to like-minded people, vicious actions, at least with respect to many characteristic vices, would be unlikely to succeed. Imagine a group of people who delight in exploiting other people. Such are likely, given sufficient time, to find their deepest desires frustrated. Surely one's foes will eventually catch on (say after a thousand or a million years). If one's desires do not find expression in (successful) action, one will be frustrated. The continued frustration of desires entails the lack of fulfillment of one's second nature. In such a situation, most people would likely go insane.

There are other objections that could be developed. Surely most people are not totally habituated to vice upon death. Their character will be an admixture of virtue and vice. The fulfillment of a single "second nature" would result in the progressive dissatisfaction of one's other vicious tendencies as well as the shrinking of one's virtuous tendencies (constituting a progressive loss of being). Moreover, deprived of the common graces of God that are essential to life, long before one approaches eternity, one's *human* being would disintegrate. The moral psychology that Stump and Dante countenance runs counter to ordinary human experience.

Conclusion

Christian doctrines of hell create a problem for orthodox theists. If God loves us like a parent loves her child, then the following are prima facie incompatible:

1. God is love.
2. There is a hell.

I have argued that (1) and (2) are incompatible on both the medieval torture chamber and the Dantean/Stump views of hell. Attempts to reconcile (1) and (2) fail.

I have predicated the argument for the incompatibility of hell and divine love on the assumption of Christianity's traditional eternal torture chamber view of hell. There are, however, nontraditional options open to the Christian theist (Crockett 1997; Hart 2019), options more fitting robust doctrines of divine love. One might, for example, reject the claim that hell is eternal; one might also reject the more severe, literal metaphors of hell as, well, metaphorical. Some Christians hold the doctrine of *annihilationism* – the view that unbelievers are punished for a finite period of time (with punishment precisely attuned to or merited by their sins) and then cease existing (this, again, is the view of some Muslims and Jews). Or one might follow Stump and hold that the punishment is psychological rather than physical (yet eternal). Or one might think, like some Muslim theologians, that the wicked are punished precisely according to their sins (and not a bit more) and, at the end of their punishment, enter into paradise. Each of these doctrines attempts to reconcile some sort of doctrine of hell with divine justice and love.

The problem of hell doesn't go away easily for Christians. I suspect that Augustine and Aquinas believed that Scripture clearly taught the doctrine of hell as (God-inflicted) eternal and unrelenting torture. Belief in such a hell was, for them, nonnegotiable. So, in order to render (1) and (2) compatible, they reinterpreted God's love. God, on their reinterpretation, loves in the mode of benevolence – God wills the good, that is, God wills all that is necessary for salvation (even if most don't embrace God's grace); if many, perhaps most, don't accept God's grace and thereby end up in hell, so be it. God did everything possible for their highest good. Moreover, God loves the damned by continuing their existence (which is a good).

Suppose, instead of holding fast to the biblical metaphors of hell, the medievals had held fast to the biblical metaphors of God's parental love. And, instead of reinterpreting divine love to make it fit with the eternal torture chamber view of hell, suppose they had reinterpreted hell to make it fit with divine parental love. They might have thought the good parent would never give up even *postmortem*, especially not after a mere three score and ten *ante mortem* (in less than optimal epistemic conditions). If so, they might have leaned more into the wiles of Omniscience and Omnipotence to lovingly attract even the most recalcitrant to God's loving self. They might have thought less of retribution and more of rehabilitation. And for the obstinate, they may have taken more seriously the good of *not to be* in hellish circumstances.

Medieval notions of love and hell make God more a sadistic torturer who keeps His victims alive just so he can maximally inflict pain than a caring parent who would with all her power never cease attempting to benefit her child through her sufferings. Julian, in a letter to Augustine opposed to Augustine's views on the original guilt of infants, contends that such a view is beneath contempt. "It would show a just and reasonable sense of propriety to treat you as beneath argument: you have come so far from religious feeling, from civilised standards, so far indeed from common sense, that you think your Lord capable of committing kinds of crime which are hardly found among barbarian tribes."[11] The same could be said, I think, for the medievals' views on divine love and their doctrine of hell.

4 Human Love

Love Divine and Human

While understanding the nature of the divine and the nature of divine love has proven difficult, understanding human love as defined in the Abrahamic holy books is not so difficult. Ease of definition, however, is not equivalent to ease of

---

[11] *Contra Secundam Juliani Responsionem Opus Imperfectum* 1.48, after Brown 1967:391. As quoted in Kirwan (1989: 134).

acquisition. It is, we'll learn from those same holy books, much easier to define love than to be loving. We'll get to that soon enough.

Whenever I tell devout Muslims, Christians, and Jews that I'm writing on love in the Abrahamic tradition, I get this response (not always in exactly these words): "Ooh, that's easy. We're supposed to love like God." God is love, they say, so love like God. I don't ask them which God – the God of Perfect-Being Theology or the God of Open Theism? I don't ask them about their views on transcendence or mention the *via negativa*. If our only access to the divine nature is through what God is not (the *via negativa*), then we have no idea what divine love is at all (except that it's not hatred, or "God is not hatred"). If God is radically transcendent, then no humanly available concepts could possibly apply to God; so we cannot meaningfully say "God is love" at all. Given the *via negativa* or radical transcendence, God is the unknowable something we know not what. Not much of a model of love.

If God is the God of Perfect-Being Theology, then God loves in the mode of benevolence. The impassible God eternally resides in a state of perpetual, undisturbable bliss. The impassible God has no sympathy or empathy, so cannot get upset if God's creatures suffer or fall into grievous sin. God's benevolence may even fit, I argued in the previous section, with the traditional Christian doctrine of hell; God's good-doing would be maximal, even if all of God's creatures were to reject God's mercies. So, even if all of God's creatures were to suffer in hell, God would be maximally loving and completely self-satisfied. The impassible God, who loves in the mode of benevolence, is unperturbed by the eternal and unrelenting suffering of the damned in hell.

Should humans then model God and God's love in the mode the of benevolence?

I remember hearing a sermon by a famous hell-fire-and-brimstone preacher. First, the preacher exulted in the suffering of those in hell (in general). At that stage of my life, I relished the fate of the damned (in general) as well, so I, like the rest of the congregation, savored his descriptions of the suffering of the damned; those in hell get what they deserve, we all thought. Smugly. But then, after a dramatic pause to take a breath, he moved from the general to the particular: "If my mother herself were to suffer in hell, it would not impinge one iota on my happiness in heaven. Indeed, her just judgment and punishment by God would contribute to my enjoyment of God's mercy in heaven." We all gasped in horror.

Our hearts were telling us what our minds could not – I cannot love my mother *and* delight in her eternal and unrelenting torture. Perhaps God can love my mother *and* delight in her eternal and unrelenting torture; I cannot. So I should not love like the impassible God.

I cannot and should not love like God, if God's highest love is benevolence, because I have desires for my mother's good, and if those desires are unfulfilled, I suffer with her and for her. My happiness depends, in part, on her happiness. This is true not just of my mother: I love my father in that good-desiring and empathetic way, too. And my brother and sister, and my wife, and my children and my friends, and members of my community and . . . .. where does it all end? What is the extent of my good-desiring, empathetic love?

If human love is good-desiring and empathetic, then the highest form of human love is compassion. And if we mourn with those who mourn and rejoice with those who rejoice, then my flourishing (happiness in the deepest sense of the term) is deeply intertwined with the flourishing of others: your good is my good, your suffering is my suffering (and vice versa).

In this section, starting with the Hebrew Scriptures, I will argue that each of the three Abrahamic traditions teaches, at their deepest levels, compassion as the highest form of human love. I will go on to argue that the three religions don't restrict compassion to kith and kin, extending it from neighbor to stranger all the way to enemy. And I will argue that the Abrahamic traditions insist on universal compassionate love as the most essential condition of the flourishing that God desires for all of the peoples of the world. But first, the problem of speaking of the Abrahamic tradition.

The Abraham Traditions

I have so far been speaking of the Abrahamic tradition as though it's possible to speak meaningfully of the Abrahamic tradition. Unlike *belief in*, which can be grounded in Abraham's initial experience of God and faithfully transmitted to succeeding generations with wide variations of *beliefs about,* traditions are systems of thought and practice that, as such, are essentially constituted by beliefs about. Yet there is no Abrahamic tradition of shared beliefs about God. If one were to ask of the intersection of beliefs held by Jews, Muslims, and Christians, the answer may be the empty set (or not). There is little overlap of beliefs among all people at all times who have identified as Muslims, Christians, or Jews. If not the empty set, the overlapping beliefs may include rather uninformative propositions about God and/ or Abraham: something like "there is an undefined divine being who created the world and said something to Abraham a long time ago." If we were to include agnostic or history-skeptical Muslims or Christians or Jews, then neither God nor Abraham would be included in the set of shared beliefs. Shared Abrahamic beliefs about God = the empty set (or a very small but not very useful set of shared beliefs).

We have already seen several deep disagreements about God between those who endorse Perfect-Being Theology and Open Theism, between those who affirm radical transcendence and those who affirm modest transcendence, between those who ascribe positive attributes to God and those who follow the *via negativa*.

We find each of these approaches within each of the three traditions and more – making it impossible, really, to speak meaningfully even of *the* Jewish tradition or *the* Christian tradition or *the* Islamic tradition, let alone *the* Abrahamic tradition. There is no set of essential beliefs affirmed by all Jews at all times, from, say, the Exodus to the Holocaust. While many conservative contemporary Christians insist that belief in the Trinity and the Incarnation are required for Christian faith, the Trinity and the Incarnation were not declared essential until centuries after the time of Jesus; moreover, many self-identified and sincere followers of Jesus have been blissfully unaware of the Councils of Nicea and Chalcedon which formulated the so-called orthodox view of the Trinity and Incarnation. I can't think of any belief or doctrine which is essential to the Christian faith from the time of the disciples to home church Christians in twentieth-century, post-Mao China. Muslims divided into Sunni and Shia soon after Mohammed's death. That's just two of the countless schools of Islamic thought – we find also Hanbali, Hanafi, Maliki, and Shafei; the Ibadis, Zayds, and Ismailis; and the Barelvi, Salafi, and Wahhabists. And more. Moreover, people within each of these subtraditions disagree about who or what is faithful to each subtradition and even how to precisely define each subtradition. Unlike the search for the most basic particle in the universe, when theologians probe deeper and deeper into each tradition, they find vastly more disagreement than consensus.

So just as it makes no sense to speak of *the* Muslim or *the* Jewish or *the* Christian tradition, it makes even less sense to speak of *the* Abrahamic tradition. Indeed, there are probably no (self-conscious) members of the Abrahamic tradition. There have been no Abrahamic councils, no Abrahamic creeds, no Abrahamic pope, and few people identify as Abrahamic believers. Most people who think of an Abrahamic tradition at all identify as either Jews, Christians, or Muslims, not Abrahamists.

I will complicate this a bit more. It would be easier to speak meaningfully of the Abrahamic tradition if there were a set of authoritative texts shared by Muslims, Christians, and Jews. But there is not.

Jews, for example, affirm the Hebrew Bible (what Christians call the Old Testament); and, while they accept that Jesus was a rabbi, Jews reject nearly the entirety of the New Testament; and since they don't consider Mohammed a Prophet, Jews reject the Quran as divine revelation.

While Christians affirm both the Old and New Testaments, their theological "takes" on the Old Testament (the Hebrew Bible) vary wildly from Jewish takes on the Hebrew Bible. Just as English professors see Christ-figures and phallic symbols everywhere in literature, Christians see Jesus everywhere in the Old Testament; where Christians see Jesus, Jews, well, do not (and not without reason). Like the Jews, Christians reject Mohammed as a prophet and, so, the Quran as revelation.

Finally, while Muslims affirm Adam, Noah, Abraham, Isaac, and Jesus as prophets, they don't accept the Hebrew Bible's or the New Testament's narratives of those prophets. Although Jesus is mentioned more times in the Quran than the Prophet Mohammed, Muslims don't accept the New Testament and reject the Trinity and Incarnation. The Quran and subsequent Islamic tradition had their own stories of Jesus.

In short, there is no common set of texts that would or could define "the Abrahamic tradition."

So, when I speak about the Abrahamic tradition on love, I am speaking of a construction from authoritative texts within each tradition. That is, I will, to the best of my ability, present *a* Hebrew Bible view of love,[12] *a* New Testament view of love,[13] and *a* Quranic view of love.[14] I don't claim that I've thereby offered *the* Jewish view of love or *the* Christian view of love or *the* Islamic view of love (because, again, I think it impossible to identify an essential Judaism, Christianity, or Islam). Finally, although I will continue to use the term for convenience's sake, I won't be offering *the* Abrahamic view of love.

Love in the Abrahamic Traditions

In Matthew 22, we read:

> An expert in religious law, asked him [Jesus] a question to test him: "Teacher, which commandment in the law is the greatest?" Jesus said to him, "'Love the Lord your God with all your heart, with all your soul, and with all your mind.' This is the first and greatest commandment. The second is like it: 'Love your neighbor as yourself.' All the law and the prophets depend on these two commandments."

In Leviticus 19, which the Jewish Jesus is surely quoting, the Lord speaks to Moses:

> "When you reap the harvest of your land, you shall not reap your field right up to its edge, neither shall you gather the gleanings after your harvest. And you

---

[12] For Jewish authors on love, see Harvey 1987, Maimonides 2000, and Goodman 2008.

[13] For Christian authors on love, see Nygren 1953, Lewis 1960, and Oord 2010.

[14] For Muslim authors on love, see Avicenna 1945, Chittick 1983, and Ghazi 2011.

shall not strip your vineyard bare, neither shall you gather the fallen grapes of your vineyard. You shall leave them for the poor and for the sojourner: I am the LORD your God. You shall not steal; you shall not deal falsely; you shall not lie to one another. You shall not swear by my name falsely, and so profane the name of your God: I am the LORD. You shall not oppress your neighbor or rob him. The wages of a hired servant shall not remain with you all night until the morning. You shall not curse the deaf or put a stumbling block before the blind, but you shall fear your God: I am the LORD. You shall do no injustice in court. You shall not be partial to the poor or defer to the great, but in righteousness shall you judge your neighbor. You shall not go around as a slanderer among your people, and you shall not stand up against the life of your neighbor: I am the LORD. You shall not hate your brother in your heart, but you shall reason frankly with your neighbor, lest you incur sin because of him. You shall not take vengeance or bear a grudge against the sons of your own people, but you shall love your neighbor as yourself: I am the LORD."

In this passage, loving your neighbor as yourself involves leaving the extras in your fields for the poor, being truthful with one another, neither oppressing nor robbing one's neighbor, paying wages promptly, caring for the disabled, and administering justice impartially. We find a similar list of the manifestations of love in the Quran:

> be good to parents and to kinsmen and orphans and the needy and the close neighbor and the distant neighbor and the companion at your side and the wayfarer ... Surely, Allah does not like the proud and boastful (4.36)

In the Hebrew Bible, The New Testament, and the Quran, we hear that love insists on kindness and compassion and fairness toward one's near neighbor, the poor and the stranger (the distant neighbor), even as you love yourself.

The Hebrew Bible, The New Testament, and the Quran affirm, in these texts and their broader contexts, love of neighbor. Self-love, they seem to assume, is easy. And it is. Kin-love, they also seem to assume, is easy. And it mostly is. I have an in-built love for my children that creates an unbreakable bond. And, though not as strong but still really strong, I have in-built bonds for my brother and sister, my parents and, extending out but weakening as it goes, for my uncles and aunts, and cousins, and second-cousins and third-cousins. I'm also pretty committed to my closest neighbors and members of my religious community. My closest neighbors and members of my religious community have proven their trust. For closest neighbors, by watching over my house when we're gone or babysitting my children (as I do for them) or sharing their lawn mower. For members of my religious community, trust is proven by attending weekly services, giving tithes, and contributing to potlucks. There's a kind of tit-for-tat-based-trust among neighbors and within religious communities.

These are all, I think, what the Quranic-text above calls "close neighbors." And love for the close neighbor is, again, fairly easy and typically mutually beneficial.

But the Abrahamic religions go much further: we must love, as the Quran calls them, the distant neighbor. This makes love much more demanding. Distant neighbors, wayfarers, the alien, sojourners – whatever each Scriptural text calls them – include members of other tribes and nations and religious groups.

Our fears of "the other" – fears resulting from competition for scarce resources, fears of strange religious practices, fears of differently colored skin, fears of being exploited or robbed or raped or even killed, fears of catching this disease or being identified with that outcast – create conditions inconducive to love of second-class citizens, the stranger and the enemy, the love on which each of the three traditions insists (Ohman 2005).

Minimally, in the Abrahamic tradition, love of neighbor means *acting* for the good of others. Concretely, we read that love of neighbor means sharing my bounty with the starving, promptly paying an honest wage for hard work, keeping promises, caring for the needy, including the outcast and dispensing goods fairly.

To be sure, the world would be a vastly better place if everyone were to love their neighbor – members of other tribes and nations, members of other religious groups, second-class citizens, the stranger, and enemy – in the sense of acting for their good.

This is, of course, love in the mode of benevolence – intending and acting for the good of others.

But the Hebrew Bible, the New Testament, and the Quran call us to aspire to a higher form of love, love as compassion. The Hebrew Bible, the New Testament, and the Quran not only call us to *act* for the good of others, they call us to *be loving* – to be compassionate, patient, generous, and forgiving.

Here's a way to put it: I love myself not only by acting for my own good, I care for myself (and care when my needs aren't met). So, loving my neighbor as myself means not only acting for my neighbor's good, it also means caring for my neighbor (and caring when their needs aren't met). It means rejoicing with those who rejoice and mourning with those who mourn. And, in felt response to their needs, to act for their joy and to relieve their suffering.

Such caring, then, involves a deeply felt concern for neighbors, one that moves us to act in empathetic and respectful responses to their needs. Again, I take "compassion" to be the best term to unite both empathy and respect with action.

The highest form of Abrahamic neighbor-love, then, is compassion – when we see our neighbor's needs and our tender hearts are not satisfied until we meet those needs.

To be clear: if you can't drum up concern for that stinky beggar or that dreaded Arab (to concede a Western stereotype), you must still love them in the mode of benevolence – you must act for their good. You can't opt out of love just because you've lost those loving feelings. But love in the mode of benevolence is more like duty-keeping than love in its highest form – compassion.

In each of the Abrahamic traditions, love in its highest form is compassion – empathy and respect-motivated action for the good of others from kin to stranger to enemy.

Empathy and Love

Each of the Abrahamic traditions, or at least each of their authoritative texts, endorses compassion as the highest form of love. Compassion, as I've defined it, is empathy and respect-motivated acts of mercy. While I've made a strong case that each tradition endorses love as acts of mercy, I don't think I've made as strong of a case for empathy. So, before addressing the difficulties of empathy, I will first address the importance of empathy in the Abrahamic texts.

While many texts in the Hebrew Bible are indicative of empathy, I will focus here on just a few that speak of love of stranger. Throughout the Hebrew Bible, we hear versions of: "You shall love the stranger, for you were strangers in the land of Egypt" (Deuteronomy 10:19). This clearly smacks of empathy toward strangers – an identification of thought and feeling because one had been a persecuted stranger oneself. Such empathy, such fellow-feeling and fellow-understanding, ground mercy for the oft-mistreated and oft-feared stranger. We also read:

- And you shall not mistreat a stranger, nor shall you oppress him, *for you were strangers in the land of Egypt* (Exodus 22:20).
- You shall love the stranger, *for you were strangers in the land of Egypt* (Deuteronomy 10:19).
- You shall not despise an Egyptian, *for you were a sojourner in his land* (Deuteronomy 23:8).
- You shall not pervert the judgment of a stranger or an orphan … *You shall remember that you were a slave in Egypt,* and the Lord, your God, redeemed you from there; therefore, I command you to do this thing (Deuteronomy 24:17-18).

Since the recalling of painful memories, which these texts intend, stirs up painful feelings, these remembrances teach that love of stranger is grounded in empathy. Painful remembrances can create empathy – identification of feeling (*emotional empathy*) and understanding of how and what it is like to be the persecuted and suffering minority in a foreign land (*cognitive empathy*). Based on shared feelings and understandings, one acts in love and justice: no mistreatment or oppression, no dehumanization, no injustice or dispossession.

The Book of Leviticus challenges the Hebrews to treat the stranger as one of their own (tribe), with all of the assumed thoughts and feelings thereof. Leviticus 19 extends compassion to the stranger: "And if a stranger lives with you in your land, you shall not do him wrong. The stranger that lives with you shall be to you as the native among you, and you shall Love him as yourself; for you were strangers in the land of Egypt: I am the Lord your G-d." Exodus 23:9 explicitly grounds love of foreigner in empathy: "And you shall not oppress a stranger, *for you know the feelings of the stranger,* since you were strangers in the land of Egypt." The heart of the ex-stranger is, or should be, moved by the suffering of the current stranger – moved by fellow-feeling and understanding to act in love and justice.

The God of the Hebrew Bible is represented as acting out of empathy on behalf of Israel while enslaved in Egypt: "I have indeed seen the misery of my people in Egypt. I have heard them crying out because of their slave drivers, and I am concerned about their suffering. So I have come down" (Exodus 3:7-8). If this is how God loves, then human beings *should* love like God.

The New Testament explores loving your neighbor as yourself the most fully of all of the Abrahamic texts: "Do unto them as you would have them do to you." I take it that the "do unto others" part, within its context, applies to both attitudes and action. We care about ourselves, for sure; that is assumed. We feel for ourselves and our situations; again, assumed. We easily excuse and forgive ourselves; again, assumed. So, if we were to love others as we love ourselves, we would seek to understand others as we understand ourselves (empathy), and be patient with and forgive others for their flaws and misdeeds (patience and forgiveness).

Even if I lack such fellow feelings for you, of course, I should not kill you, I should not steal your possessions, and I should keep my promises. The New Testament permits no moral vacations or exceptions. But again, such benevolent good-doing is more like duty or justice than love.

Love in the highest degree (of the as-I-love-myself variety) moves one by fellow-feeling and understanding to invite the stranger into one's home, offer them friendship, share their burdens, relieve their suffering, forgive their transgressions, be patient with their shortcomings, and show them kindness.

The model of God for Christians is Jesus, believed to be the visible image of the invisible God. Jesus, in the Synoptic gospels, grieves, cares, and weeps over people and their situations. In the parable of prodigal son (Luke 15:11-31) we read that the father "filled with compassion" for his lost son runs out, throws his arms around him and kisses him. We read repeatedly in Matthew and Luke that Jesus acted because he was moved by compassion (Matthew 9:36, 14:14; Luke 7:13, 10:33, 15:20). Moved by compassion, Jesus acts – healing the sick, comforting the weary, liberating the oppressed, and including the outcast. If Jesus is God, then we should love as God loves: empathy-motivated acts of mercy.

As Muslims around the world and throughout time are inclined to do, I will start with reflection on the one God. After all, Muslims start and end their day with God, ritually repeating the beginning and the end of the Quran:

> In the name of God (Allah), the Compassionate (*al-Rahman*), the Merciful (*al-Rahim*).

As noted in Section 1, every chapter of the Quran but one begins with this resounding affirmation of God's mercy; "compassion" and "mercy," again share the same root, *r-ḥ-m* (ر ح م), which connotes tender mercy, gentleness, lovingkindness, pity, and compassion. Words that share the root *r-ḥ-m* – "compassionate" (raḥmān), "compassion" (raḥmān), and "showing compassion" (raḥmān) – occur 326 times in the Quran. And when Allah acts, Allah's actions are rooted in Allah's affection and concern for His children. If this is what Allah is like, then we should love like Allah.

When Muslims pray, five times each day, to God (Allah), the Compassionate, the Merciful, they are ritually connecting to the Source of Compassion and Mercy. To those who submit to the Compassionate, the Most Merciful gives love/affection:

> Those who believe and do righteous deeds, the Most Merciful will give them love (*wuddan*) (19.96)

Wuddan, a synonym for "love" in the Quran, is often translated as "affection" or "desire" indicating the affective, empathetic dimension of love. God then empowers the believer, from the inside as it were, to empathy-driven acts of mercy.

I could go on exegeting the Hebrew Bible, the New Testament, and the Quran, but I'll stop. I think I've made the case that the highest form of love in each tradition is compassion. Moreover, I've tried to show that, taken literally, each of their authoritative texts represents God's highest form of love as compassion. And, if those representations of God as compassionate are true, then we should love like God.

Problems of Love Human

When I was considering this Element in this Problems of God series, I intended to discuss the problem of human love for God. I decided, instead, to focus on the problem of biblical love of humans for humans. Such are problems enough.

I had intended to discuss the problem of total devotion – the demand to love God with all of our heart, soul and strength. If one were to love God with all of one's heart, how could there possibly be any heart-room left over for love of anyone else, including any other human being? Some claim that Soren Kierkegaard's decision to break off his engagement with his beloved Regina Olsen was due to his desire for complete devotion to God. For him, faith in God came down to this choice: either complete devotion to God or love of Regina Olsen. Kierkegaard's understanding of Christianity meant choosing God and, like Abraham with Isaac, sacrificing his relationship with the earthly human he most deeply loved. Evidently, Regina believed Kierkegaard sacrificed her to God.

I think the problem of total devotion is a serious and fascinating problem (Adams 1986). But I've decided not to discuss it here. If you are interested, you can take it up as homework!

One might think that the problem of total devotion is an abstract theological problem of interest only to geeky philosophers. Many readers probably think that some, perhaps most, theological problems are so abstract, so disconnected from life, so irrelevant to faith that no reasonable person should waste their time on them. They might recall, "can God create a stone so great He cannot lift it?" and "how many angels can dance on the head of a pin?" as prime examples of such problems. While I don't think such problems have much existential oomph, I qua geek philosopher do find them interesting and have spent more time thinking about them than I dare publicly admit (OK, really just the stone/ omnipotence problem; the angels/pin problem is too geeky even for me).

In this final section, I've determined to consider a problem that I take to be of monumental existential import.

While I think the problem of total devotion has some existential import (though I don't feel its weight nearly as profoundly as Kierkegaard did), I think that the problem that I will discuss is existentialer (while I concede this is not a word, it should be). The problem I will discuss concerns *the possibility of empathy*. The difficulty of cultivating empathy (make no mistake, it is extremely difficult) makes love of others, as commanded in the Abrahamic traditions, difficult or even impossible.

The Impossibility of Empathy?

It's hard to love like God. Probably no surprises when put that way. Let me put it another way: it's hard to live up to Abrahamic love-as-compassion.

I've been trying to write in a way that is engaging and inviting. I've wanted to bring the reader along on this project to understand love within three great religious traditions. I've tried to fairly but firmly portray the deficiencies of love as benevolence (at least for human beings, if not for God). And I've tried to make attractive the idea of love as compassion (at least for human beings, if not for God).

But, and here's the kicker, universal compassion is nigh impossible for humans. Again, another way of putting it: each of the three Abrahamic traditions call us to love neighbor, stranger and even enemy, and while humans might be ok-ish at neighbor-love, we are not well-constituted for stranger or enemy love. Indeed, we may be evolutionarily opposed to strangers and enemies.[15]

By insisting on love as compassion (for the entire world), God may be asking the impossible.

God, who is essentially omnipotent and essentially love, may so love the world, but finite and frail human beings do not, and maybe even cannot. How, we might wonder, do we get there from here?

Let me briefly state the empirical importance of empathy and then return to its difficult cultivation.

Empathy and Justice

The chant, "No justice, no peace," which may have originated with Martin Luther King, Jr., has been widely heard. Recent studies in the social sciences suggest that we should take one step further back: "No empathy, no justice." Without empathy, one lacks the sensitivity to be aware of and/or feel the need to respond to injustice (Decety 2016). The higher a person is on various empathy scales, the more likely they are to recognize injustice. In order to perceive injustice, one needs to move beyond self to grasp how vicious actions feel to others. Without being able to put ourselves into their shoes (or lack of shoes as the case may be), we are unlikely to act on their behalf. If I cannot identify with their pain and suffering, then I am unlikely to see the injustice. And so, I am unlikely to expend any effort to relieve it (or to think it worth relieving).

No empathy, no justice.

Consider a common belief and corresponding practice until the nineteenth century: the belief that some group is naturally disposed to be slaves; to get more specific, the belief that black Africans are more animal than human, and, as such more suited to menial than mental tasks; moreover, the belief that the flourishing of members of that group requires them to be mastered and submissive. While you, in the twenty-first century may be appalled at images of poorly treated black slaves (and you should be), very few eighteenth-century

---

[15] For a discussion of the difficulties concerning empathy, see Baron-Cohen 2011, Bloom 2016, and Bazelgette 2017.

Americans were (even when seeing such treatment face-to-face). Many people, perhaps nearly all in communities of slave-keepers, who saw slaves chained and bought and sold and whipped and separated from their children or parents, felt no empathy. As a result, few Americans worked to free slaves. Lacking empathy, they could not see the injustice. Not seeing the injustice, they didn't act to relieve it. Moreover, they (the slave-owners and their surrounding communities) lacked cognitive empathy – they did not consider slaves to be fully human; so, they lacked identification with them as humans. Their ignorance dehumanized slaves, "justifying" their mistreatment (Smith 2012). And their lack of empathy and respect prevented them for recognizing the injustice. Seeing no injustice, they did not insist on justice.

No empathy, no justice.

But "no empathy, no justice" isn't just true of nineteenth-century Americans. It's true of everyone. It's true of you and me. Let me explain this autobiographically so you don't feel judged. I suspect my lack of empathy for, say, beggars prevents me from giving beggars a dime. Neuroscientific studies show that when people like me are shown photos of dirty beggars we have disgust reactions, not empathy (Bradshaw 2019). Because I feel disgust and no empathy for beggars, I don't give that beggar any money. I suspect my lack of empathy for members of Black youth gangs prevents me from protesting historical social conditions that perpetuate Black poverty. I suspect my lack of empathy encourages me to see all Latinos as lazy Mexican and discourages me from seeing them as God-loved refugees fleeing danger and death in the home countries. Finally, I suspect that my lack of empathy for Pakistanis contributes to my laissez-faire attitude to global climate warming (though one-third of Pakistan was recently flooded causing massive loss of property and life).

I could go on, but I hope each reader feels what the science shows – no empathy, no justice.

So, if Muslims–Christians–Jews are committed, as God is, to justice rolling down like waters and righteousness like an ever-flowing stream, then we all need to work a lot harder and even together to muster up some empathy.

The problem of empathy: it's hard for me to work up empathy for people outside of my own family or friends. So it's difficult for me to work hard to relieve the pain and suffering of those outside of my family and circle of friends.

And if I'm right, cultivating empathy for out-group is hard for you, too.

Why Is It So Hard to Cultivate Empathy?

I believe the difficulty of cultivating empathy, especially for distant neighbors, strangers, and enemies lies in our inordinate love of self. The further a group of persons is from one's self, the more difficult it is to cultivate empathy and so extend compassion (Sibley and Barlow 2016). I believe this is rooted in our evolution-shaped psychology but will mostly ignore that here. I will simply describe how our devotion to self, as we move out from self to others, makes the cultivation of empathy difficult (maybe, in some cases, impossible).

Devotion to self – self-love – is not in itself bad. After all, without self-love one might think that one needs to sacrifice all of one's desires for the good of others. The desires for, say, food and drink, clothing, and shelter, to love and be loved, a relationship with God, and a meaningful life are good, and their satisfaction contributes to human flourishing. So, it is OK to attend to the satisfaction of those desires. Of course, such desires can at times be excessive – we can become gluttons, for example, or greedy. Moreover, one can inordinately prize one's own desires over everyone else's – for example, by breaking promises or by stealing. And everyone has illegitimate desires – for their neighbor's wife, say, or their donkey. But taken in moderation and given due sensitivity to the needs of others, a person can properly satisfy their legitimate desires as a means to a flourishing life. Self-love is OK

Self love is problematic, however, when it becomes inordinate, that is, when one's self is one's exclusive concern to the detriment of others.

I think exclusive concern for self is often rooted in fear of others. For example, since early human tribes, for hundreds of thousands of years, were often in competition with other tribes, sometimes for scarce resources, running into someone from another tribe could elicit instinctive fear. Suppose a hundred thousand years ago, one were to see a stranger across a field. Thoughts race, or could race, through one's mind. Does the stranger want that deer that I'm hunting? Are they coming to steal some stored food? Do they want to take a young woman from our group as a mate? Or do they want to trade or share in the hunting and split the bounty? Early humans would need to make snap judgments – is that person from another tribe friend or foe? Probably, more often than not, members of another tribe were foe. Fear.

Given such very real fears concerning competitive others, one's first reaction to this fearful situation would have been very likely, fight or flight. While such fears might conduce to aggression, hoarding, territoriality, and even fighting, they scarcely conduce to empathy (Richins 2021). Fear crowds out any room in one's heart for empathy (Dolder 2016).

Now suppose we expand from concern for self to concern for family. I believe we are evolutionarily hard-wired to have deep concern for our own offspring. A human's deep desires for the good of their offspring create opportunities for massive neuro-bathings of positive dopey things (oxytocin) in a parent's brain (Scatliffe 2019). Literally, parents biochemically suffer when their children suffer and biochemically rejoice when their children rejoice. A parent will give up food, sleep, and even life itself for the good of their child. Parent–child empathy, according to contemporary neuroscience, is (fairly) easy and easily (evolutionarily) explained.

When we expand our circle out to our tribe (our near, nonkin neighbors), we mostly expand out to people who look, act, and believe a lot like us. And it's not so hard to love another me. Early human tribes were not large – maybe thirty-five to seventy-five and were grounded in both blood and mutual, earned trust; tribes might be better considered extended kin groups or even extended families (in both literal and metaphorical senses).

But make no mistake: except for one's children, who get a free genetic pass, the other members of one's tribe need to earn and preserve their trust. Humans require fairly regular assurance that everyone in their tribe is on the same team (can be trusted). We are sensitive to so-called *costly signals* that prove trust and commitment to the mutual good of the group (McAndrew 2019). Costly signals might be routine and simple – like singing and dancing together, or sharing excessive food to those who lack. Or costly signals might be rare and difficult – like sacrificing a bull to the gods or enduring a painful coming-of-age ritual. But self- and kin-loving humans need to be constantly reassured that they can trust other members of their own group.

Constantly proving and needing trust are not good breeding grounds for the cultivation of empathy. The need to prove trust suggests that we have deep-down fears even of members of our own tribe. Such fears may explain our addiction to gossip – we need to regularly and easily gather information about people in our group to constantly assess who's in (good) and who's out (evil) (McAndrew 2007).

Such fears may also explain scapegoating – in times of misfortune that cause feelings of fear, a member of one's tribe may be blamed and sacrificed (kicked out of the group). A single person, if they've violated the group trust, may be blamed for all of the group's problems and sent into exile (or punished or treated very badly). The origins of the term "scapegoat" are found in the Hebrew Bible where the Israelites ritually placed all of their sins onto the head of a literal goat, which was driven into the wilderness to carry the people's transgressions out into desolate land (Leviticus 16). While the punisher or group of punishers may feel better and more righteous by transferring all of their blame onto the scapegoat, such fear-motivated self-righteousness toward various individuals or groups is scarcely conducive to the cultivation of empathy (Landes 1994).

Scapegoating likewise applies to the in-group's blame of out-groups for their misfortunes. Historically, Jews have been convenient targets for scapegoating. Medieval Europeans blamed them for the bubonic plague and twentieth-century Nazis blamed them for a host of Germany's social ills. Such in-group, out-group scapegoating can manifest in racism, prejudice, bigotry, and nationalism. Again, enemies of empathy.

One's group, we know, defines the boundaries of in and out, light and dark, good and bad, friend and enemy, victim and scapegoat. Jane Elliott's famous blue-eye, brown-eye experiment shows how easy it is to both (a) identify as in-group and (b) take on in-group values – in-good/out-bad. (Bloom 2005). Over fifty years ago, she divided her Iowan students, who were all white, by eye color; then she told the children that people with brown eyes were smarter, faster, and cleaner than those with blue eyes. Within hours the brown-eyed children began mistreating the others, and the blue-eyed children began underperforming academically. Everyone quickly learned that in-group is good, out-group is bad. In such in-group/out-group valu-ations lie the seeds of tribalism, segregation, division, and even death. But not empathy.

Because of our inordinate commitments to self, kin, and tribe, empathy for out-group others is extremely difficult to cultivate (Cikara 2011). As I've argued, the further away one gets from one's self and kin, the more difficult it is to overcome the fears that crowd out empathy. We are considerably more fearful of nonkin members of our tribe than we are of kin, of distant versus near neighbors, of out-group over in-group, and of enemies over friends. The further out, the less like us someone is, the greater the potential for empathy-preventing fear.

The less we know about others, the more likely we are to prejudge them by their inclusion in a group. As a white, middle-class, American Christian – I am likely to view non-whites, lower and upper classes, non-Americans, non-Christians as stereotypical members of their groups. As such, I may make hasty judgment about "them Mexicans" and "them Arabs" and "them Muslims." In so doing, I will ascribe stereotypical and typically demeaning and dehumanizing attributes to members of those groups (Smith 2012). Mexicans are lazy, Arabs are barbaric, and Muslims are violent.

Studies show how pervasive and intractable such stereotypes can be (Nosek 2007). Suppose you are, like me, a white, middle-class, American Christian and you were to read an article titled "Mexicans are not lazy, Arabs are not barbaric and Muslims are not violent" that goes on to decisively refute those stereotypes. If you were to initially accept those stereotypes, we know two things. First, you would not see the "not" in the sentences above – that is you would see in your mind, despite the indelible text on a page, "Mexicans are lazy, Arabs are barbaric and Muslims are violent." Your prejudices don't allow you to see evidence against your prejudices (Hakim 2020). Second, the presentation of evidence would, likely, make you more extreme and more dogmatic (Lord 1979). Humans, it seems, have an in-built evidence-insensitivity device when it comes to their deepest biases. Evidence makes us retreat back into our often-deadly prejudices.

And if no empathy, then we cannot see injustice. And if we cannot see injustice, we won't work to achieve justice (Decety 2016).

No empathy, no justice.

Love in the mode of compassion requires extending from self to home to community to world.

This is the problem: God commands us to love the world, but we seem psychologically incapable of loving the world.

Maybe it's even worse. Maybe religion makes us more tribal and less likely to love the world.

Sadly, the Abrahamic religions seem to contribute to making the world more tribal, more in-group, more nationalistic. Jews are persecuting Muslims in the West Bank; Muslim terrorists hate America; US Christians condoned the unjust 2002 attack on Iraq and don't care about the 500,000 to 1,000,000 innocent Arab lives lost as a result of the war. We all build walls and deploy bombs. Islam, Judaism, and Christianity can seem to be little more than tribal markers to identify who is in and who is out and to justify the mistreatment of those who are out. Contemporary Abrahamic religions, it seems, contribute more to deadly in-group than to extending love to the outcast, the stranger and even the enemy.

The God who calls us to love has been turned into an idol to justify our fears and hatreds.

Not to understate: this is a problem.

Love and Hope

Each of the three Abrahamic traditions affirms God's plan for love-directed justice to flourish throughout the world. Is there any reason to think or at least hope that Judaism, Christianity, and Islam are helping or could help God achieve God's plan for the flourishing of love-directed justice in the world?

Each of the three Abrahamic traditions offers "plans" for the cultivation of empathy. The first of these plans is for faith to tie people heart-to-heart to the Compassionate, the All-Merciful. There are different terms in each tradition to describe this transformative power – grace, favor, *baraka*, *kiddush*, salvation, sanctification, *tazkiyah* – but they all point to ways that God connects His creatures to His loving self. God, then, is the originating power source of empathy flowing out through God's creatures to the world. Faith or belief connect one to empathy's power source.

The second plan involves *rituals of love,* aimed at cultivating empathy. I will mention just one from each tradition.

Islam's daily prayers is a ritual aimed at both unselfing and at God-connecting; in prostrating and proclaiming devotion to the One God, the Compassionate and the all-Merciful, the Muslim seeks both to affirm that he or she is not God and to connect with God's empathic power.

The Jewish sabbath is a similar unselfing exercise. Once a week, for twenty-four straight hours, devout Jews cease from creating to connect to the true Creator. Moreover, the ritual practice of joining with kin and community to share in a worship service and a Shabbat meal creates bonds well beyond the self; within the Jewish community, one learns to love beyond the self and kin.

Finally, the Christian virtue of hospitality includes caring and concern, in the form of food and shelter, for strangers and even enemies.

We find each of these rituals of love – unselfing prayers, communal sharing, and hospitality – in each of the Abrahamic traditions.

How psychologically effective are these plans for universal love and empathy-motivated justice? While the jury is still out because the studies are relatively new, the evidence suggests that various religious beliefs and ritual practices can cultivate empathy (even in atheists!) (Mercadillo 2017). Prayer can move a person out of their self toward God (humility) and out of their self toward their community and even beyond their community (generosity and empathy) (Cline 1965; Herzog 2020). Prayer can make us more inclined to forgive (Fincham 2017), less vengeful (Bremmer 2011), and more likely to cooperate with others (Lambert 2013). "Studies show," as they say, that connecting with God – loving God – can transform people from self-centeredness to others-centeredness.

Let me skip right to hospitality. Studies on training to overcome and prevent biases through various trainings or seminars, on which companies and organizations have spent billions, are discouraging. There seem to be no long-term effects of anti-bias training on, for example, racism or sexism (Dobbin 2018). Indeed, there seem to be few short-term effects. Only one thing seems to change people's deeply rooted negative attitudes toward out-groups – personal contact (Binder 2009). The only way to overcome bigotry, racism, and nationalism is to become friends with someone from another religion or race or nation. You can't overcome bigotry, racism, and nationalism by reading a book or attending a week-long bias-reduction workshop. You can, however, overcome bigotry, racism, and nationalism by cultivating and practicing the virtue of hospitality – by building a bridge, opening a door, sipping coffee, or sharing a meal – by taking the risk to turn a stranger into a friend.

Prayer and hospitality aimed at friendship may be love's only hope for this world.

Conclusion

If God is the God of Perfect-Being Theology, then humans should not love like God. If God is the God of Open Theism and if the God of Open Theism loves in the mode of compassion, like a father his children, then humans should love like God – the whole world (not just kith and kin), like God. Humans should love the whole world in empathy-motivated, injustice-alleviating action, like God.

But, if the empirical studies on the cultivation of empathy are right, it's darn hard to love like God. Empathy is increasingly elusive the further one gets from one's self.

Moreover, God is infinite and we are finite. God so loves the world, but we finite creatures love just one person at a time. So God's plan for compassion-seeking-justice involves (1) love of God (connection with the empathy power source) and (2) rituals of love (to transform us from self-centeredness to others-centeredness). The rituals of love include, among many other unselfing practices, prayer, communal gatherings, and hospitality. Each successful step requires overcoming the various fears that crowd out empathy, confessing that the further out we go from self, the greater our fears of others. So we need to pray for and cultivate the virtue of courage to take that first step down our street to invite our very different neighbors into our home, with no expectation of reward or conversion. Hospitality, after all, aims at friendship.

If, if, if, then, then, then. Lots of "ifs," lots of "thens." Lots of clarifications and qualifications and concerns. No decisively solved problems. Lots of problems.

What is the sober truth about God and love?

I have no idea.

But if there is a God of Compassion who wants us to love like God, then humans need to connect with the all-Merciful, sincerely practice the rituals of love within their Muslim or Jewish or Christian communities, and build empathy bridges out to the world, courageously creating friendships, one person at a time.

References

Adams, Marilyn McCord. 1993. "The Problem of Hell: A Problem of Evil for Christians." In Eleonore Stump and Norman Kretzmann, eds., *Reasoned Faith: Essays in Philosophical Theology in Honor of Norman Kretzmann*. Ithaca, NY: Cornell University Press, 301–327.

Adams, Robert Merrihew. 1986. "The Problem of Total Devotion." In Robert Audi and William Wainwright, eds., *Rationality, Religious Belief, and Moral Commitment*. Ithaca, NY: Cornell University Press, 169–194.

Aquinas, Thomas. 1948. *Summa Theologica*, translated by the Fathers of the Dominican Province. New York: Benziger.

Aquinas, Thomas. 1975. *Summa Contra Gentiles*, translated by Anton C. Pegis. Notre Dame, IN: University of Notre Dame Press.

Augustine. 1950. *City of God*, translated by Marcus Dods. New York: The Modern Library.

Avenanti, Alessio, Angela Sirigu, and Salvatore M. Aglioti. 2010. "Racial Bias Reduces Empathic Sensorimotor Resonance with Other-Race Pain." *Current Biology*, 20, 1018–1022.

Avicenna. 1945. "A Treatise on Love by Ibn Sīnā," translated by Emil L. Fakhenheim. *Medieval Studies*, 7, 208–228.

Baron-Cohen, Simon. 2011. *The Science of Evil*. New York: Basic Books.

Bazalgette, Peter. 2017. *The Empathy Instinct: How to Create a More Civil Society*. London: John Murray.

Binder, Jens, et al. 2009. "Does Contact Reduce Prejudice or Does Prejudice Reduce Contact? A Longitudinal Test of the Contact Hypothesis among Majority and Minority Groups in Three European Countries." *Journal of Personality and Social Psychology*, 96(4), 843–856.

Bloom, Paul. 2016. *Against Empathy: The Case for Rational Compassion*. New York: Ecco Books.

Bloom, Stephen. 2005. "Lesson of a Lifetime." *Smithsonian Magazine*. September.

Bradshaw, Hannah, Jeff Gassen, and Sarah E. Hill. 2019. "Beggars Can't Be Choosers: Disgust as a Cue and Signal of Social Status." *OSF Preprints*, February 18.

Bremner, Ryan H., Sander L. Koole, and Brad J. Bushman. 2011. "Pray for Those Who Mistreat You: Effects of Prayer on Anger and Aggression." *Personality and Social Psychology Bulletin*, 37, 830–837.

Chittick, William. 1983. *The Sufi Path of Love: The Spiritual Teachings of Rumi*. Albany, NY: State University of New York.

Cikara, Mina, Emile G. Bruneau, and Rebecca R. Saxe. 2011. "Us and Them: Intergroup Failures of Empathy." *Current Directions in Psychological Science*, 20(3), 149–153.

Cline, Victor and James Richards. 1965. "A Factor-Analytic Study of Religious Belief and Behavior." *Journal of Personality and Social Psychology*, 1, 569–578.

Craig, William. 2000.*The Only Wise God: The Compatibility of Divine Foreknowledge and Human Freedom*. Eugene, OR: Wipf and Stock.

Creel, Richard. 1985. *Divine Impassibility: An Essay in Philosophical Theology*. Cambridge: Cambridge University Press.

Crockett, William, ed. 1997. *Four Views on Hell*. Grand Rapids, MI: Zondervan.

Decety, Jean and Keith Yoder. 2016. "Empathy and Motivation for Justice: Cognitive Empathy and Concern, but Not Emotional Empathy, Predict Sensitivity to Injustice for Others." *Social Neuroscience*, 11(1), 1–14.

Dobbin, Frank and Alexandra Kalev. 2018. "Why Doesn't Diversity Training Work? The Challenge for Industry and Academia." *Anthropology Now*, 10 (2), 48–55.

Dolder, Patrick C., Yasmin Schmid, Felix Müller, Stefan Borgwardt, and Matthias E. Liechti. 2016. "LSD Acutely Impairs Fear Recognition and Enhances Emotional Empathy and Sociality." *Neuropsychopharmacology*, 41, 2638–2646.

Dolezal, James. 2011. *God without Parts: Divine Simplicity and the Metaphysics of God's Absoluteness*. Eugene, OR: Pickwick.

Fincham, Frank D. and Ross W. May. 2017. "Prayer and Forgiveness: Beyond Relationship Quality and Extension to Marriage." *Journal of Family Psychology*, 31(6), 734–741.

Flint, Thomas. 1998. *Divine Providence: The Molinist Account.*, Ithaca, NY: Cornell University Press.

Frame, John. 2001. *No Other God: A Response to Open Theism.*, Phillipsburg, NJ: Presbyterian & Reformed.

Fretheim, Terence. 1984. *The Suffering of God: An Old Testament Perspective*. Minneapolis, MN: Fortress.

Gavrilyuk, Paul L. 2004. *The Suffering of the Impassible God: The Dialectics of Patristic Thought*. Oxford: Oxford University Press.

Geisler, Norman. 1997. *Creating God in the Image of Man*. Minneapolis, MN: Bethany House.

Geisler, Norman and H. Wayne House. 2001. *The Battle for God: Responding to the Challenge of Neotheism*. Grand Rapids, MI: Kregel.

Ghazi bin Muhammad. 2011. *Love in the Holy Qur'an*. Islamic Texts Society.

Goodman, Lenn. 2008. *Love Thy Neighbor as Thyself*. New York: Oxford University Press.

Grant, W. Matthews. 2019. *Free Will and God's Universal Causality: The Dual Sources Account*. New York, NY: Bloomsbury Academic.

Hakim, Nadir H., Xian Zhao, and Natasha Bhar. 2020. "The Paradox of the Moderate Muslim Discourse: Subtyping Promotes Support for Anti-Muslim Policies." *Frontiers of Psychology*, December 21, 1–10.

Hart, David Bentley. 2019. *That All Shall Be Saved: Heaven, Hell, and Universal Salvation*. New Haven, CT: Yale University Press.

Harvey, Steven. 1987. "Love." In Arthur Cohen and Paul Mendes-Flohreds, eds., *Contemporary Jewish Religious Thought* . New York: Scribners, 557–563.

Hasker, William. 2004. *Providence, Evil, and the Openness of God*, Routledge Studies in the Philosophy of Religion. New York: Routledge.

Helm, Paul. 1990. "The Impossibility of Divine Passibility." In Nigel M. de Cameron, ed., *The Power and Weakness of God*. Edinburgh: Rutherford House Books, 119–140.

Helm, Paul. 1994. *The Providence of God*, Contours of Christian Theology. Downers Grove, IL: InterVarsity Press.

Herzog, Patricia Snell, et al. 2020. "Religiosity and Generosity: Multi-Level Approaches to Studying the Religiousness of Prosocial Actions." *Religions*, 11(9), 1–46.

Heschel, Abraham Joshua. 1962. *The Prophets*. Jewish Publication Society of America.

Hick, John. 1985. *Problems of Religious Pluralism*. London: Macmillan Press.

Hume, David. 1980. *Dialogues Concerning Natural Religion and the Posthumous Essays*, edited and introduced by R.H. Popkin. Indianapolis, IA: Hackett.

Kirwan, Cristopher. 1989. *Augustine*. London: Routledge.

Kripke, Saul. 1980. *Naming and Necessity*. Oxford: Blackwell.

Kvanvig, Jonathan. 1993. *The Problem of Hell*. New York: Oxford University Press.

Lambert, Nathaniel and Steven Beach. 2013. "Shifting toward Cooperative Tendencies and Forgiveness: How Partner-Focused Prayer Transforms Motivation." *Personal Relationships*, 20(1), 184–197.

Landes, Richard. 1994. "Scapegoating." In Peter N. Stearn, ed., *Encyclopedia of Social History*. New York: Garland, 859–860.

Lewis, C. Staples. 1960. *The Four Loves*. London: Geoffrey Bles.

Lord, Charles, Lee Ross, and Mark Lepper. 1979. "Biased Assimilation and Attitude Polarization: The Effects of Prior Theories on Subsequently Considered Evidence." *Journal of Personality and Social Psychology*, 37(11), 2098–2109.

Maimonides, Moses Ben. 2000. *The Guide for the Perplexed*, rev. ed., translated by Michael Friedlander. Mineola, NY: Dover.

Matts, Robert and A. Chadwick Thornhill, eds. 2019. *Divine Impassibility: Four Views of God's Emotions and Suffering*. Downers Grove, IL: IVP Academic.

McAndrew, Francis. 2019. "Costly Signaling Theory." In Todd Shackelford and Viviana Weekes-Shackelford, eds., *Encyclopedia of Evolutionary Psychological Science*. New York, NY: Springer International Publishing, 1525–1532.

McAndrew, Francis, Emily Bell, Contitta Maria Garcia. 2007. "Who Do We Tell and Whom Do We Tell On? Gossip as a Strategy for Status Enhancement." *Journal of Applied Social Psychology*, 37(7), 1562–1577.

Mercadillo, Roberto E., Juan Fernandez-Ruiz, Omar Cadena, Emilio Domínguez-Salazar, Erick H. Pasaye, Javier Velázquez-Moctezuma. 2017. "The Franciscan Prayer Elicits Empathic and Cooperative Intentions in Atheists: A Neurocognitive and Phenomenological Enquiry." *Frontiers in Sociology*, 2, 22.

Mullins, Ryan T. 2020. *God and Emotion*. Cambridge: Cambridge University Press.

Naomi, Scatliffe, Sharon Casavant, Dorothy Vittner, and Xiaomei Cong. 2019. "Oxytocin and Early Parent-Infant Interactions: A Systematic Review." *International Journal of Nursing Sciences*, 6(4), 445–453.

Nosek, Brian, et al. 2007. "Pervasiveness and Correlates of Implicit Attitudes and Stereotypes." *European Review of Social Psychology*, 18(1), 36–88.

Nygren, Anders. 1953. *Agape and Eros*, translated by Philip S. Watson. London: S.P.C.K.

Ohman, Arne. 2005. "Conditioned Fear of a Face: A Prelude to Ethnic Enmity?" *Science*, 309(5735), 711–713.

Oord, Thomas Jay. 2010. *Defining Love: A Philosophical, Scientific, and Theological Engagement*. Grand Rapids, MI: Brazos Press.

Oord, Thomas Jay. 2022. *Pluriform Love: An Open and Relational Theology of Well-Being*. Grasmere, ID: SacraSage Press.

Pinnock, Clark. 2001. *Most Moved Mover: A Theology of God's Openness*. Grand Rapids, MI: Baker Books.

Pinnock, Clark H., Richard Rice, John Sanders, William Hasker, and David Basinger. 1994. *The Openness of God: A Biblical Challenge to the Traditional Understanding of God*. Downers Grove, IL: InterVarsity.

Richins, Matt T., Manuela Barreto, Anke Karl, and Natalia Lawrence. 2021. "Incidental Fear Reduces Empathy for an Out-Group's Pain." *Emotion*, 21 (3), 536–544.

Rogers, Katherin A. 2000. *Perfect Being Theology*. Edinburgh: Edinburgh University Press.

Sanders, John. 1998. *The God Who Risks: A Theology of Providence*. Downers Grove, IL: InterVarsity Press.

Sibley, Chris and Fiona Kate Barlow, eds. 2016. *The Cambridge Handbook of the Psychology of Prejudice*. Cambridge: Cambridge University Press.

Smith, David Livingstone. 2012. *Less Than Human: Why We Demean, Enslave, and Exterminate Others*. New York, NY: St. Martin's Griffin.

Stump, Eleonore. 1986. "Dante's Hell, Aquinas's Moral Theory, and the Love of God." *Canadian Journal of Philosophy*, 16(1986), 181–198.

Stump, Elenore. 1993. "Aquinas on the Sufferings of Job." In Eleonore Stump, ed., *Reasoned Faith*. Ithaca, NY: Cornell University Press, 335–336.

Stump, Eleonore and Norman Kretzman. 1981. "Eternity." *Journal of Philosophy*, 78(8), 429–458.

Swinburne, Richard. 1983. "A Theodicy of Heaven and Hell." In Alfred J. Freddoso, ed., *The Existence & Nature of God*. Notre Dame, IN: University of Notre Dame Press, 37–54.

Swinburne, Richard. 1993. *The Coherence of Theism*, rev. ed. New York: Oxford University Press.

Talbott, Thomas. 1999. *The Inescapable Love of God*. Eugene, OR: Wipf and Stock.

Vorauer, Jacquie and Stacey Sasak. 2009. "Helpful Only in the Abstract? Ironic Effects of Empathy in Intergroup Interaction." *Psychological Science*, 20(2), 191–197.

Walls, Jerry. 1992. *Hell: The Logic of Damnation*. Notre Dame, IN: University of Notre Dame Press.

Ware, Bruce. 2001. *God's Lesser Glory: The Diminished God of Open Theism*. Wheaton, IL: Crossway Books.

Weinandy, Thomas. 2000. *Does God Suffer?* Notre Dame, IN: University of Notre Dame Press.

Williams, Rowan. 2021. *Understanding and Misunderstanding "Negative Theology."* Marquette, WI: Marquette University Press.

Wolterstorff, Nicholas. 1988. "Suffering Love." In Thomas V. Morris, ed., *Philosophy and the Christian Faith*. Notre Dame, IN: University of Notre Dame Press, 196–237.

Portions of Section 1 are drawn from

Clark, Kelly James. 2008. "A Tale of Two Deities." *American Theological Inquiry*, 1(2), pp. 8–25.

Clark, Kelly James. 2015. Muslims and Christians: On Worshipping the Same God, *Huffington Post*. December 28.

Portions of Section 2 are drawn from

Clark, Kelly James. 1992. "Hold Not Thy Peace at My Tears: A Methodological Discussion of Divine Impassibility." *Our Knowledge of God*. Kluwer Academic, 167–193.

Clark, Kelly James. 1997. "Knowing the Unknowable." *Books and Culture*: https://www.booksandculture.com/articles/1997/sepoct/7b5029.html.

Portions of Section 3 are drawn from

Clark, Kelly James. "God is Great, God is Good: Medieval Conceptions of Divine Goodness and the Problem of Human Suffering." *Religious Studies*, 37, 15–31.

Cambridge Elements ≡

The Problems of God

Series Editor

Michael L. Peterson
Asbury Theological Seminary

Michael Peterson is Professor of Philosophy at Asbury Theological Seminary. He is the author of *God and Evil* (Routledge); *Monotheism, Suffering, and Evil* (Cambridge University Press); *With All Your Mind* (University of Notre Dame Press); *C. S. Lewis and the Christian Worldview* (Oxford University Press); *Evil and the Christian God* (Baker Book House); and *Philosophy of Education: Issues and Options* (Intervarsity Press). He is co-author of *Reason and Religious Belief* (Oxford University Press); *Science, Evolution, and Religion: A Debate about Atheism and Theism* (Oxford University Press); and *Biology, Religion, and Philosophy* (Cambridge University Press). He is editor of *The Problem of Evil: Selected Readings* (University of Notre Dame Press). He is co-editor of *Philosophy of Religion: Selected Readings* (Oxford University Press) and *Contemporary Debates in Philosophy of Religion* (Wiley-Blackwell). He served as General Editor of the Blackwell monograph series Exploring Philosophy of Religion and is founding Managing Editor of the journal *Faith and Philosophy.*

About the Series

This series explores problems related to God, such as the human quest for God or gods, contemplation of God, and critique and rejection of God. Concise, authoritative volumes in this series will reflect the methods of a variety of disciplines, including philosophy of religion, theology, religious studies, and sociology.

Cambridge Elements $\equiv$

The Problems of God

Elements in the Series

A full series listing is available at: www.cambridge.org/EPOG.

Printed in the United States
by Baker & Taylor Publisher Services